SOLD

HOW TOP REAL ESTATE AGENTS ARE USING THE INTERNET TO CAPTURE MORE LEADS AND CLOSE MORE SALES

KEN LAPP & DAN LOK

ISBN: 978-0-9964460-1-3

TABLE OF CONTENTS

INTRODUCTION

"We can save a bundle on property taxes if we move to Cyberspace and live at our web address."

lthough the internet has been around for a long time, to many people it's still new. They don't understand it. Even people who've used the internet for years miss some of the most basic concepts. This book explains them and how to make money with them.

I encourage you to pay particular attention to the sections that talk about Specialization. You'll find this topic discussed thoroughly and objectively. There are many concepts fundamental to success in internet marketing in this book, but this is the most important one.

If you're reading this book it means you are determined to be successful, ready to take action, and willing to research to find the right course of action. You are not at all like Stephen Leacock's fabled hero who jumped on his horse and "rode madly off in all directions".

It's easy to get distracted, as they say "to have the shiny object syndrome". But you don't. I would even go so far as to say that the simple fact that you are reading this book means you'll be successful. I'm not trying to claim this book will be the sole reason for your success. You will undoubtedly find many sources of good information that will help you on your way.

However, this book could be one of the main reasons for your success. That is my goal.

This book is the result of 16 years success in Internet Marketing and a lifetime passion for effective communication. I hope you find the explanations clear and the tone casual and easy to read.

My intention is that this book can be an effective resource for real estate agents in different situations:

- those who are new to internet marketing

- those who understand parts of it and want to understand the whole picture

- those who want to do it themselves

- those who want to be involved but want some help with the difficult parts

- those who want it done for them but want to understand what's going on

And finally, I need to say something about industry terminology.

"Internet Marketing" in common usage means any kind of marketing efforts that have to do with the internet. When

I use the term I mean a combination of getting high rankings on Google so prospects will come to your website, and having a website that will persuade perfect strangers to contact you.

"Search Engine Optimization" or "SEO" as it's often abbreviated, talks the tasks necessary to get high rankings on Google for your website. Some of those tasks involve changes to your website, while others are done on other websites. So you can see where there might be some overlap between the two terms. It's just part of the business.

And when we say the "Organic" listings on Google we simply mean the normal listings of websites on the search results pages, that is, listings on the Search Results pages that are not paid, not ads.

When someone goes to Google and types a word or phrase into the search box, that phrase is called a keyword, or a keyword phrase. When we say "Google's algorithm" we mean the criteria Google uses to decide what rankings to give your website.

The word "blog" is very confusing. A blog can be a separate entity like a website or it can just be a part of a complete website. The word "blog" is also used to describe an article written and published on blog. So your blog can have many blogs on it. A "blog article" can also be described as a "blog post". But "post" can also be a verb. When an article is published on a blog we can say a blog has been posted to your blog.

Although it's not technically correct, it's common usage to use the words "Internet" and "world wide web" interchangeably. We do it in this book because we like to explain things using common language.

I hope this book serves you well.

Ken Lapp

JOIN OUR FREE WEBINAR AS A COMPANION TO THIS BOOK –

★ Register Now due to limited number of participants – Go to http://www.topagentinternetmarketing.com/FreeWebinar

"How Top Real Estate Agents are Using the Internet to Capture More Leads and Close More Sales"

- See more Real Life Examples

- Learn Advanced Strategies

- Watch the actual concepts and processes described in this book done for you live

- Qualify for a Free One-on-One Consultation ($500 value)

- Enter your name for a Free Website Analysis ($1,200 value)

CHAPTER 1
HOW TO MAKE YOUR WEBSITE SELL

© Randy Glasbergen / glasbergen.com

"Opportunity texted me, tweeted me, linked to me, friended me, blogged me and spammed me. I was expecting it to knock!"

Actually what you want is opportunity to come to your website, in the form of qualified prospects. Your website is the best place to pique their interest, educate them, convince them you're the one to deal with, and get them to contact you.

This chapter talks about how to make a website that will do that. You can have all the traffic in the world coming to your website, but if it doesn't get prospects to contact you all your work is wasted.

And let's be clear. We're not talking about your friends and neighbours. We're talking about complete strangers. Your website has to convince them to trust you and contact you. That's how to make money on the internet.

This chapter talks about having a feed from an MLS® System on your website, about the advantages of a custom WordPress website, about what a website needs in order to get high rankings on Google, and to convince prospects to contact you.

This chapter also talks about how to get the best testimonials, and clears up the misconceptions many real estate agents have about using the words REALTOR® and MLS® System. Using them incorrectly can get you in trouble.

A. What is MLS® System IDX? Do You Need It?

IDX stands for Internet Data Exchange. It enables MLS® System listings to be on your website, and updated automatically as new ones are added and old ones removed. New rules that will come into effect in 2016 say that the 850 MLS® Systems in the United States have to update their listings every 12 hours instead of every 3 days like they do now.

Your website will be a more useful resource for prospects if it has listings from your local MLS® System. Depending on your website provider you can usually have as many "Saved Searches" as you like, which will automatically display all current listings, for example, for "condos in (neighborhood) between $300,000 and $500,000" with a single click.

There are many companies throughout the United States and Canada that will provide local MLS® System IDX for your website for a fee of $50 or $60 a month. They're easy to find.

B. Why a WordPress Website is the Best

Although there are many companies that provide templated websites for real estate agents we recommend a custom WordPress website for a number of reasons:

1. **Google loves WordPress**
   WordPress started out many years ago as blogging software, and Google loves blogging. Since then the open source community of computer programmers has made WordPress into an excellent website development software. Most small business websites are now built with WordPress.

2. **Easy-to-use Content Management System**
   The WordPress system to manage the content on your website pages, called the Content Management System (CMS), is as easy to use as Microsoft Word. We can train our clients in 15 minutes on the phone.

3. **Limited access for your protection**
   You can have "admin" access to your website if you wish. But it means you can accidentally delete the wrong code and damage your website beyond repair. This creates unnecessary downtime and expense because your website has to be rebuilt almost from scratch.

   However, with WordPress you can use only "editor" access, which means you can add, delete, and change text and photos on any page, and even pages themselves, but you can't accidentally damage the website.

4. **Easily structure the pages and links**
   When Google analyzes the pages on your website to determine what rankings they should have, one

of the things they look at is the structure and the URLs of the pages. The WordPress CMS allows you to easily rearrange the page structure and change the URLs any way you want them. Templated website systems do not.

In this case I'm talking about which pages of your website are linked to which other pages of your website. These are called Internal Links. Google looks at how the pages are linked to each other to determine which pages are the most important. If one page has many supporting pages under it all talking about the same topic, that page is more likely to receive higher rankings for that topic.

5. **Separate page for each of your personal listings**
   It can be a good strategy to make it so when people search on Google for the address of one of your personal listings, the dedicated page for that listing on your website ranks first. We need to write more text on your dedicated page than is mentioned in the MLS® System.

   However, doing this is not a guarantee your page will rank first. The ranking of individual pages on your website is greatly dependent on the overall ranking of your website.

6. **Access to HTML code**
   You need access to the HTML code in the Head section of your website pages in order to make changes that are very important for your rankings on search engines. A custom WordPress website gives you complete access. It's best not to work

with the background code of your website unless you know what you're doing. Better to hire somebody who does.

Although some template website systems do provide access to the code of the website pages, many do not. We can't work with clients who deal with those companies.

7. **Mobile**

There are a number of good plugins available for WordPress that can be used to inexpensively make your website fully responsive. "Responsive" is the best kind of mobile website. It looks and works the best on any size screen. Photos and graphics automatically reduce in size to fit, the text enlarges, and buttons become larger for fat fingers.

Companies that provide template websites either don't provide any mobile website, or the mobile website they provide is not as good looking and as functional as a fully responsive mobile website.

C. What Should Your Website Look Like?

When prospects come to a website for the first time they decide at a glance, even before they know they've decided, if the agent is successful, skilled, knowledgeable, a good person, whether they can trust this agent, and whether or not they will be satisfied with their service. So your website must be professionally designed. It must be beautiful. The colors, shapes, photos, text and designs must work together to convey all the above values at a glance.

But if you want to make money from your website it must be more than beautiful. It has to sell. This means it must be designed by internet marketing professionals. Many designers can build a beautiful website, but only internet marketing professionals can build a website that sells.

Part of the responsibility of internet marketing professionals is to keep up with what people expect from websites. The way people use the internet is changing all the time. In order to build effective websites internet marketing professionals have to put the right information in the right places so that prospects get their questions answered, so they trust you, and so they contact you.

1. **Branding**

   Branding yourself is an important part of marketing for a real estate agent, as long as it's not all you're doing. And you have to do it right. For real estate agents good branding means:

   1. **The Look**

      Having a distinctive look to your website that you carry forward in everything you do – your social media accounts, your email signature, your business cards, brochures, and all other advertising. If everything you do has the same look each individual marketing piece has more impact on prospects because they remember they've seen your brand many other places.

   2. **Specializing**

      Branding can also mean specializing in a particular segment of the market. Prospects won't believe you are an expert in too large an area. For example, there are 39 neighborhoods in Vancouver, BC. Who will believe you're an expert in "Vancouver real estate"?

But if you say you are an expert in real estate near the University of British Columbia, one of the neighborhoods in Vancouver, anyone would believe you, especially if you show them you have passion for that neighborhood, and tell them why UBC is the BEST neighborhood in Vancouver. More about Branding and Specialization in the next section.

D. Crucial Characteristics of a Website That Sells

1. Put your best foot forward

If prospects get a good feeling from "The Look" of your homepage they scroll down to see what else they can learn about this agent, and to find answers to their questions. In internet marketing you need to put the most important, the most interesting, the most persuasive reasons to do business with you in the top half of your homepage.

I've heard too many people say "I put the most interesting points on the About Us page (or some other page) because I want people to click into my website." This is exactly the wrong approach. If you don't put the most interesting reasons to deal with you right on your homepage people will never see them. You only have a few seconds to catch their interest or they'll be gone. They'll go to another website.

2. Must Be Easy To Read

The text on your website must be easy to read. On most websites that it's not. Designers who are more interested in making a website beautiful than in making it work, often have text that is small and light grey. That's absolutely ridiculous. Many people have vision problems, especially middle aged people who are more likely to be able to afford real estate.

The 2011 American Housing Survey by the US Census says that the typical home owner is 54 years old. (source – realtor.org) And even if a particular prospect doesn't have vision problems, marketing is about making it as easy as possible for people to get your message. Making your text small and light grey makes it harder to read. That's just the opposite of what we're trying to do. It's a question of beauty vs function.

Having website page text that is easy to read means:

a. It should be black.

b. It should be large enough to read easily.

c. It should contain plenty of headings and sub-headings for skimmers.

d. No paragraphs longer than 4 or 5 lines.

e. Bullet points wherever possible, with an empty line between each point.

f. Bolded text once in a while. But be careful, because too much bold text is actually harder to read.

g. A small photo here and there to add colour and interest. Nice colors in a photo will make the page more visually appealing, and people are drawn to look at photos of people, especially if the person in the photo is looking at them.

E. Seven Ingredients that Must Be On Your Homepage

An important thing to note here is that you don't need to worry about your homepage being long. The longer the better, actually, as long as it's well-written, interesting, and easy to read.

1. What you do and where you do it

This is the first information people look for on a website. Nobody wants to spend 20 minutes looking around your website only to find you don't do what they want, or service their area. This information is usually best right at the top of the page on the left beside the logo.

For real estate agents 'what you do' is usually obvious from your logo or the name of your broker. I mention this here just a cautionary note to put, for example, something like "Mary Smith Real Estate Services − Specializing in (your area)" instead of just "Mary Smith".

2. Your photo

This is a place where you can't afford to be too humble or shy. It doesn't matter at all what you look like. All that matters is that you look friendly and professional. So put on your best suit, and tie (for men), visit a professional photographer with a studio of her own, sit on a stool, and get her to take at least 50 shots of you in different sitting positions with different smiles.

Smile - Please understand that you MUST smile. No matter who you are, no matter who your customers are, you will get more people calling you from your website and you'll do more business if you smile.

If you have a friendly smile it means you're approachable. Having your photo on the homepage makes the whole website seem personal instead of corporate. And once you've chosen a photo to use on your website use it also on your social media accounts, and in all your advertising. Make it a part of your personal brand.

3. **Your Specialization**
As in many other areas of business, if you spread limited resources too thinly on the internet you get nothing. Rather than going for all the marbles, there are a number of benefits to going after a smaller group of marbles, that is, of Specializing in a particular area.

Your website will have higher rankings on Google which will result in more traffic to your website without a massive investment. And when people come to your website many more of them will want you to be their agent.

So next you need to talk about what makes you different from your competitors. And of course, what makes you different is your Specialization. You brand yourself as "The (your area) Specialist", and fill your website with content about your area that is as interesting as possible. Try to give it the slant that (your area) is the best place to live. You will get more listings and make more money if you become (your area's) greatest booster, its champion.

More Listings – You'll get more listings because all the people who live in your area will see you love this area as much as they do. You will obviously sell the area and their home with passion. That's the kind of agent everybody wants selling their home.

More Buyers – You'll get more buyers because when buyers come to your website they'll see that you know everything there is to know about that area. You'll be able to find them just the home they're looking for because you know where it is. They'll probably ask you which areas of your neighbourhood you like the best and why. But of course, that depends on what they're looking for.

4. **Video**

   If you have a video of yourself talking on your homepage people can get to know you before they call. They can judge for themselves whether or not you are professional, knowledgeable, and some-body they can be comfortable with. It doesn't have to be a long video. Even 30 seconds are enough. A video like this can help establish and reinforce your personal brand.

   There are many other reasons to use video on your website:

   i. Google will rank YouTube.com videos

separately from your website in their organic search results, so your name and one of your marketing tools can be on the first page of Google one more time in addition to your website. It's more impressive so more prospects will visit your website.

ii. It's great to have a video of you showing the audience the features you love about your neighbourhood, your area of Specialization.

iii. If you do a video of one of your listings people can take a tour of the home from 10,000 miles away. Be sure to show only the best points in the video. Leave the audience wanting more information.

iv. Video testimonials are very powerful. See below for more on this.

5. **Trust Signals**

You're going to get a lot of complete strangers coming to your website if you have good rankings on Google, so it's good to have as many reasons to trust you on your homepage as possible.

Trust signals can be things like:

a. A testimonial, with a clickable link "More Testimonials" to your Testimonials page. You could even have a video testimonial on your homepage with a link to your Testimonials page underneath it.

b. You can also talk about the number of

years you've been in business, and the number of clients you've worked with over the years. Use specific numbers even if they're a low estimate. Specific numbers are much more credible.

c. It's important to talk a bit about the community service work you do. Every real estate agent should do some kind of community service in their area of specialty, even if it's just donating some cash once a year. But it's much more powerful if you have a small photo on your homepage of you smiling and flipping flapjacks at the local pancake breakfast, for example.

d. This shows you know your area of Specialty. It shows that the people in your area are good people, and that you are friendly and approachable so they don't need to be afraid of you, that you won't be arrogant or make them feel stupid.

e. More importantly, it implies that the people in your area trust you. This means you have good morals and ethics. You are honest, so strangers can trust you.

f. Logos of awards you've won as a real estate agent can also be trust signals. It's good to say something like "These awards demonstrate I'm a professional, and that you'll always receive award winning service from start to completion."

g. You can also use logos of professional associations you belong to.

6. **What Happens Next**

It's good to have a quick statement telling people
what happens next after they call you. It helps take
the fear of the unknown out of the situation. And
it helps people know that you are a professional
who has a system that works, and you've done this
successfully many times before.

It could be something simple like "The first thing
we'll do is discuss your needs and make sure all
your questions are answered. Then I'll explain my
proven 12 point process and we'll make a plan to
accomplish your goals."

7. **Call to Action**

It's best if every page on your website has some
kind of Call To Action. It can be anything from a
small form offering special information to a simple
line of text with a link to your Contact Us page
saying "Please contact me for more information".

F. Your Blog

In addition to having a lot of content on your website about your area of specialization Google will recognize
your website as more of an authority if you are constantly
adding new content. The best way to add new content is
with your blog. Please see the Introduction to this book
for an explanation of basic blogging terminology.

We literally write hundreds of high quality articles
about issues and events that are happening in our clients'
areas every month. These articles need to be original con-

tent, not copied from any other website, and not used on any other website after yours.

Each blog article should have one of your keywords in the title, in the Description Meta Tag, and usually only once in the text of the article. Each article should have a relevant photo, a link to another page on your website that has content related to the issue in the blog article, and it should have a call to action inviting people to contact you for more information.

You can buy stock photos sometimes for $1 to $3 from websites like Stockfresh, Fotolia, and iStockPhoto. We've included much more about blogging in Bonus Chapter 2 – Blogging For Profit.

G. Your Testimonials Page

It's important to have a Testimonials page on your website. As mentioned above, there's no such thing as too many testimonials. People are highly influenced by social proof. The same way we want to go to a restaurant that's always full, we want to deal with real estate agents who have a lot of testimonials.

The most important thing about testimonials is to do as much as you can to show they are real, because some unscrupulous agents write fake testimonials for their website.

The most persuasive are video testimonials because website visitors can judge for themselves whether the person in the video is an actual client or one of your drinking buddies. The next persuasive are photo testimonials. Just the fact that there's a photo of a person they've never seen before gives website visitors more of a feeling it's authentic.

The easiest to fake are plain text testimonials, but they are still good, and the more the better. So we encourage all our clients to ask every one of their customers for a testimonial. Some real estate agents are hesitant to ask. Here are some ways to make asking easy and more productive.

i. **How To Ask for Email Testimonials**

The easiest way to ask for a testimonial is to say to clients something like "Mary, if you feel like it I'd sure appreciate a few kind words in an email sometime. It would really help me." And smile. Every reasonable client will say they'd be happy to help you out.

If a few days or weeks go by and it seems clear they have forgotten, you can send them an email saying something like "Hi Mary, If you have time I'd sure appreciate that testimonial we talked about. Thanks so much. It will really help me. If you're too busy or not sure what to say some of my clients ask me to write a few words in their name and send it to them for approval. Please let me know what you prefer."

If you still don't hear back in a few more days just write a few words as if your customer was writing it and send it to her, saying something like:

"Hi Mary, Thanks so much for agreeing to let me put a few kind words from you on my website. It will really help me. I know you're busy so I've gone ahead and put a few words up. Please have a look and let me know if everything's OK. Here's the link where you can see it."

If you don't hear back just leave it on your website, and print a copy of your email to them and keep it in their file, so you have proof that you did go through the requesting process like a professional.

ii. How To Ask for Photo Testimonials

A photo testimonial is the same as above except that it has a still image beside it of the person giving the testimonial. It adds more credibility, and makes it seem more genuine.

All you have to do is, when you've asked them and they've said "Yes", take out your camera or smartphone and say something like "You know, it will really help if I can put a small photo of you smiling beside your testimonial. Would that be OK?"

The only important thing about this photo is that it will be completely unusable if they don't smile. So you may have to same something funny and take a number of quick shots. If you have one you like it's best to show it to them right then and there, to avoid them being bashful or shy later and saying they don't want that photo on your website. Tell them you need a natural looking photo.

iii. How To Ask for Video Testimonials

A video testimonial is the jackpot. If they agree to a photo you can say something like "You know the absolute best thing is a short video of your comments or feelings or anything you feel like saying. Is there anything you could say right now? It would really help me a lot. I'd sure appreciate it." Of course you can't force people or it won't be a good testimonial. You'll be able to gauge how they're feeling.

And of course the best time to ask is when you've just told them the 'subjects' have been removed on the offer they accepted, or if they're a buyer, that their offer has been accepted – sometime when they're very happy. It's always good to give clients good news in person, if you can, and have your video camera ready.

Even if you can't be there in person 'to deliver the baby' many clients will be happy to say something nice in a video later. You'll have many opportunities to pay them a personal visit.

All their friends and relatives will want to see their video on your website. They might even give you all the email addresses if you offered to send everybody the link for them.

When adding a testimonial to your website or any of your marketing materials it's best to just include the person's first name and last initial. Nothing else, such as the city or neighbourhood. Some people who aren't familiar with the internet are afraid of being contacted by weirdos or con artists. Listing names this way will allay their fears.

H. Clearing Up Confusion About Using REALTOR® and MLS System on Your Website

1. REALTOR®

In the United States you can only use the word

REALTOR® to signify your membership in the NAR, the National Association of Realtors. In Canada it's the CREA, the Canadian Real Estate Association. And even if you are a member you must always put the word in all upper case, that is, in all capital letters, and put the small "R" with a circle around it immediately after the word.

2. **MLS® System**
The CREA owns the trademark for "MLS® System" in Canada. The abbreviation "MLS" should never be used in Canada except in the phrase "MLS® System". In the United States the NAR has no such requirement.

I. Conclusion

In this chapter we learned how to make a real estate website that sells. We learned about having MLS® System IDX on your website, why a custom WordPress website will make you more money, about branding for a real estate agent, what should be on the homepage of your website and how to display it so strangers will trust you and contact you.

We learned how to ask for testimonials, and about using REALTOR® and MLS® System in any of your marketing materials.

In the next chapter we learn more about Google's ranking criteria and how to use it so Google wants to rank your website at the top of page one.

JOIN OUR FREE WEBINAR AS A COMPANION TO THIS BOOK –

★ Register Now due to limited number of participants – Go to http://www.topagentinternetmarketing.com/FreeWebinar

"How Top Real Estate Agents are Using the Internet to Capture More Leads and Close More Sales"

- See more Real Life Examples

- Learn Advanced Strategies

- Watch the actual concepts and processes described in this book done for you live

- Qualify for a Free One-on-One Consultation ($500 value)

- Enter your name for a Free Website Analysis ($1,200 value)

CHAPTER 2
A STAMPEDE OF FREE TRAFFIC TO YOUR WEBSITE

Copyright 2005 by Randy Glasbergen.
www.glasbergen.com

GLASBERGEN

**"Our new website is www.eggsalad-armpit.com
All of the good names were already taken!"**

A good domain name will help you get higher rankings on Google and more traffic to your website. It's not always possible to get a perfect one but it's usually possible to do better than eggsalad-armpit.com. ☺ Like so many things it's a ranking factor, but not a major ranking factor. More about domain names later in this chapter.

This chapter will show you how to mine Google for the best opportunities. We'll give you specific steps on how to find an area with untapped potential that will bring hundreds of prospects to your website every month. And we'll show you how to get to the top of Google for that area.

Being at the top of page one of Google not only brings large numbers of prospects to your website, an added benefit is that people think you're the best. People trust Google. When your website is at the top people think Google has determined you are the best in your field.

This chapter talks a little about how real estate agents and home buyers and sellers use the internet. It talks a lot about Google, how it works, its ranking criteria, how to use Social Media to generate leads, and the ranking criteria for Google My Business, with the red dots on the map.

In addition we talk a bit about Specialization. It's the key to making money on the internet. We talk about why it's so powerful, a little bit about the myth that you will lose business from other areas, and about how to pick your specialization both from the lead generation and the sales point of view.

We show you facts and figures about why being on page one of Google is not enough. You need to be at the top of page one of Google. And we talk about how brokers can also benefit from specialization.

A. Real Estate Prospects Using The Internet

87% of people in the United States use the internet. 93% in Canada. Internet usage is growing in both countries, and in fact, in every country in the world. (source - InternetLiveStats.com) When most people have a question, any question, the quickest and easiest way for them to find the answer is to "Google it".

The National Association of Realtors® in the United States is always studying and releasing information on real estate, on their members, and on the internet. They recently did a joint study with Google that said 90% of house hunters search the internet during their home buying process, and that real estate related internet searches are increasing every year. According to internal Google data they rose 253% on Google.com over the last four years. (source - inman.com)

The study also showed that 20% of real estate related searches were on mobile devices, which was a 120% increase year over year. Use of tablets to search online for real estate increased 300% over the year before. These are phenomenal increases. To keep up, your website must look good and work well on any size mobile internet connected device.

B. Google – Be Careful What You Believe

There is so much false information on the internet about how to get good rankings on Google. If you're doing your own research you have to be very careful what you read. One reason is that some people will say anything to get attention and traffic to their website.

Another reason is that internet usage is constantly changing. What people used to expect from a website two or three years ago is much different than what they expect now.

The most important reason why you have to be careful what you read is that Google's ranking criteria has changed so drastically. Most of the information on the internet about how to get high rankings is old and completely wrong. Things that would get you good rankings a year ago will get you penalized today.

Although it's a lot of work to keep up we actually don't mind because Google is getting better. They're better at being able to discern which websites are authorities in their field. And in the long run this makes the internet a better place.

C. How Google Makes Money

We have to put ourselves in Google's shoes for a minute. This first thing to understand is that the more people who use Google, the more money Google makes. Google makes 98% of their 50 billion dollars a year income from their AdWords, that is, their pay-per-click ads.

When more people use Google, more people click those ads. Every time somebody clicks one of those ads Google makes anywhere from a few cents to a few dollars. Pay-per-click advertising is discussed more fully in Chapter 9.

Google's strategy to get more people to use their search engine is to make it the best search engine on the internet, and they've always done a very good job. In the United States 75 to 80% of people use Google. (source - http://www.forbes.com/sites/roberthof/2015/01/08/why-googles-search-market-share-loss-to-yahoo-means-pretty-much-nothing/) In Canada it's closer to 85%.

D. Why Has Google Been So Successful?

The most important reason why Google is the most used search engine is that they are good at showing people websites that answer their questions, and doing it quickly.

To show them quickly Google has written a computer program called Googlebot, which is constantly looking at every website on the World Wide Web, and sending information about those websites back to Google to be stored in its memory banks. That way when somebody goes to Google and searches, it doesn't have to search the internet, it just search its memory banks.

Long ago Google developed their own proprietary technology for memory banks, a way of connecting many computers together, that enables them to search their memory banks very quickly and bring up links to websites that are relevant to what each particular person searched for. But, as mentioned above, to be the best search engine you have to be more than just fast. You have to be the best at showing people websites that answer their questions.

Google's method has two parts. The first part is to understand what people are actually looking for when they type in different phrases into the search box. For example, if somebody types in the word "hammer" in the search box they could be looking for at least three or four completely different things.

The second part is to bring up links to websites that are an authority in that field, that contain a lot of valuable information on whatever that person is searching for.

When somebody goes to Google and types a phrase in the search box Google looks through every website in their memory banks and brings up the ones that are an authority in that field, that relate most closely to that phrase. Google has many criteria to decide which websites are more relevant than others, and which website is the most relevant of them all.

E. How To Get Google Working For You

Of those real estate agents who have a website only a small percentage of them are getting leads from it. For most it's simply an online brochure. If you use the internet well you'll have an unfair advantage over your competition. The way to use your advantage well is to get Google working for you. Google wants to rank your website high if it is an authority. Choose an area you want to specialize in and make your website an authority on that area. Add lots of useful information about that area to your website.

If you choose the right area you can completely dominate it. Huge numbers of qualified prospects actively searching for your service will come to your website every month. This chapter will show you how to do that. But don't be disappointed. If you don't jump in and dominate the area you want now, someone else might get there before you. In marketing it always pays to be first.

The most important influence on your rankings is your website content, and how well it relates to the phrase somebody just typed into the Google search box. In the SEO industry we call this "Relevance". When somebody types a phrase into the search box Google's ranking algorithm looks for websites in its memory banks where the content of the entire website is relevant to that phrase.

Did you catch that phrase in the last sentence "the entire website". It's so important. For your website to get top rankings on Google your entire website must be talking about your area, and only about your area. I can't stress this enough.

F. Google's Ranking Criteria

After "Relevance" mentioned above, these are some of the other important criteria Google looks at to determine where to rank your website:

1. Backlinks

A backlink is a link on any other website, that if somebody went to that website, saw the link and clicked it, they would be taken to your website. If that backlink is on a high quality website that has content relevant to your website, and if the backlink is on their page in the right way, Google will take it as a sign that your website is an authority in your field and will raise your rankings.

However, if the backlink is on a low quality website without content related to yours and not on the page in the right way Google will penalized your rankings. After Relevance, the Backlinks pointing to your website are Google's second most important ranking criteria.

2. **Technical Issues**
   There are a number of technical issues we need to address on your website to tell Google what area your website is an authority in. For example, it's important to have your keywords in your Title Tag, the URL of some of your website pages, the Heading, and in the body text of the pages. But if you mention your keywords too many times Google will penalize your rankings.

3. **The Age of Your Website**
   Google knows how long your website and domain name have been live on the internet. The longer the better, so they feel you are a good, well run business.

4. **Exact Match Domain Name**
   If one or more of the words being searched for at the time match some of the words in the domain name of your website Google will assume your website has content on that topic and give you higher rankings. Ideally your domain name is short so it's easy to type and remember.

It's best if it's a .com, but if you can only get a .net or .pro with your keywords in it go for that. Having your personal name in your domain name probably won't make you any money, and it means there is less room for keywords.

5. **Click Through Rate**
When Google shows the link to your website on a search results page, if more people click on the link to your website compared to other websites on the same search results page, Google will assume your website is more attractive to people searching for that phrase. So they'll give your website higher rankings for that phrase.

6. **Traffic**
Google knows how many people visit your website. If you have a lot of people visiting your website Google takes it as a sign your website is an authority in your field.

7. **Interaction**
If visitors are staying on your website a long time and interacting with things like surveys and leaving comments on your blog posts, Google will take it as a sign that your website is more interesting, and therefore more of an authority.

G. Social Media for High Google Rankings

For Google rankings for small websites it's not necessary to get heavily involved in social media. The minimum you should have is a Facebook, Twitter, and a Google+ account. Your profile pages on those websites should be filled out completely, and visually branded to look something like your website. Google+ is very important for your rankings because of the verification processes they offer.

As a minimum amount of social media activity it's good to automatically publish the blog posts from your website on your social media accounts. It's also important that the Name, Address, and Phone number (NAP) of your business is formatted exactly the same on your website and other places on the internet as it is on your Google+ account.

H. How To Use Social Media To Get Leads

In addition to working on social media to improve your website rankings you can also use it as an independent source of leads. However, unless you know what you're doing you can spend a lot of time on social media and not get anything in return. The NAR says 91% of REALTORS® use social media to some extent. For various reasons, we suspect that some REALTORS® prefer engaging on social media to meeting prospects in person.

However, proper and consistent use of social media can definitely bring a return. Here are some tips:

1. Set up a Facebook Business Page rather than using your Personal Page.

2. Behave like you would at a cocktail party. Listen and talk about others for a long time before you start talking about yourself. It's good to post useful information twice a day for a few months before you start posting a new listing once in a while.

3. Post and tweet about information that home sellers, buyers, or even home owners might find useful or interesting.

4. Post information that would be of interest to people living in your area of specialization. That's probably where you get most or all of your clients.

5. If you don't have time to write great articles yourself you can post articles from others as long as you give them credit and link back to the original article.

6. On Twitter you can tweet about local events you support.

7. Use hashtags about your neighbourhood or area of specialization.

8. Don't ever buy likes or followers.

9. Don't try to be active on every social media website. Pick one or two and become a regular.

10. A few minutes a day will be enough as long as you do it every day.

11. If you can use a camera or Photoshop, Instagram or Pinterest can be good social media sites to attract interest in your properties or area of specialization. Instagram can be good to show photos of you behind the scenes in your everyday business, helping with staging, volunteering in your neighbourhood, showing a nice property, etc.

12. You can see more about this topic in Bonus Chapter 1 – Social Media For Real Estate Agents.

I. Why Your Description Tags Are So Important

Although Google does not use the Description Meta Tag that's on your website pages to calculate your rankings anymore, from a marketing point of view it's one of the most important parts of the page, especially your homepage. This is because when Google brings your website up as one of the websites in their search results your Description Tag is the text under the link to your website.

It's the text people read to decide whether to come to your website or not. Your Description Tags need to be the most well-written, the most compelling marketing text on your pages, talking about the most exciting and interesting reasons to visit your website.

J. Ranking Criteria for Google My Business (Red dots on the map)

This feature of Google's is very important to Local Businesses because it's an opportunity to jump to the top of page one of the search results more quickly than in the regular organic listings. Google has changed the name of this feature many times. It used to be called Google Places, Google Local, and Google Plus Local, written as "Google+ Local".

Here we're talking about the listings Google often displays on page one of the search results for phrases that include a place name, such as New York, or Vancouver. We call it the "Seven Pack" because most of the time Google displays seven websites in that group. Google My Business listings are organic, that is, not ads.

The Seven Pack websites each have a red dot with an upper case letter inside that corresponds to the same red dot showing their location on the map at the top right of the page. Google's criteria for ranking these Google My Business listings is different but related to their criteria for ranking websites in the regular organic listings.

These are some of the more important ranking criteria for Google My Business: (source - Moz.com)

1. The physical location of your office is in the place name that was included in the keyword being searched for.

2. When your Google My Business account was set up the proper Category for your business was selected. This is important. You can find the best Google My Business category for your website by searching on Google for your most important keyword phrase, and looking at the Category of the website that's currently number one in the Seven Pack.

3. The name, address, and phone number (NAP) of your business on your website is formatted the exact same way everywhere on the internet where it's mentioned, including on your website.

4. The NAP of your business is on good quality, high authority websites.

5. There is a keyword related to your business in the title of your Google My Business account. But don't doctor the title of your Google My Business account artificially to include a keyword. Google will find out eventually, and they don't like it.

6. If your website has high rankings in the Google Organic rankings your Google My Business listing will be more likely to have high rankings in the Seven Pack.

K. More Free Google Traffic From Specialization

You've probably been told many times by your broker and in training courses that specialization is one of the keys to success in real estate. Google has made that truer now than ever before. Specialization is the fastest way to get to the top of Google organic search results. If you do it right it will bring hundreds of actively searching prospects to your website every month.

It's easier to get high rankings on Google if you specialize in a smaller area because there are less websites trying to rank for that area. There's less websites fighting for the top spots. You need to have many pages on your website with high quality information about your area. Ideally, every page on your website has information that ties in with your area of specialization.

That way when people search on Google for information on your area Google sees your website as more "relevant" than other websites that have information on many areas. We'll talk more about "relevance" later. It's Google's number one ranking criteria. If Google sees your website as an authority they want to rank your website high when somebody searches for that area.

But what area should you specialize in? For real estate agents this is the secret to success in internet marketing. In this section we'll spell out the answer.

L. The Myth That Specialization Will Hurt Your Business

Some agents feel if they specialize in one area they'll lose business from other areas. But actually the opposite is true.

What we're talking about here is hundreds of complete strangers who are actively looking to sell or buy homes in your area of specialization, coming to your website directly from Google and calling you every month. You'll start getting leads from your website and making more deals. Your business will increase. You'll have more happy customers, more testimonials, and more referrals.

People who are happy with your service won't just refer you to their friends in your area. They'll refer you to their family and friends all over town. Their family and friends will do business with you because you were referred by someone they trust, and because you are an expert in real estate. Soon you'll be getting more business from all areas of town than you ever did before, all because you specialize in being an expert in one area.

M. How to Pick Your Specialization

As mentioned above, the quickest and most efficient way to increase the leads and sales you get from your website is to rank high on page one of Google for one area. But what area to pick? And how small or large should it be?

The answer has two parts:

1. The first part is that it's best to choose an area that doesn't have an agent with a good website ranking high in it already.

2. The second part of the answer is about your goals. Let's assume that your goal this year is to do an additional two ends a month from leads you get from your website. So, the area you pick to specialize in should have a large enough number of people searching for it on Google every month so that if they came to your website and contacted you, you'd be able to close at least two of them.

You have to ask yourself how many qualified prospects do you usually talk to before you close a deal. Let's say that number is 10. So, if you want to close an extra 2 deals a month you need to talk to 20 new qualified prospects.

But some prospects are more serious than others. To be conservative let's make a goal for your website of bringing you 50 new qualified prospects per month every month. You'll be able to separate the serious prospects from the time-wasters on the phone very quickly.

You can find out how many prospects are searching for any area by using the Google Keyword Planner. More about that just below. That's the way to pick an area of specialization from an internet marketing point of view.

To pick an area of specialization from a real estate sales point of view you might want to consider these points:

1. Ideally you're looking for a geographic area, a town, a municipality or county, a neighbourhood, some region that is well-known by name to everybody in the area. Or it could be a segment of the market, such as "downtown condos", but we recommend a geographic area.

2. Look at the quality of the neighbourhood. Do you like the neighbourhood? Do you know something about it? What's the crime rate? The number of listings and sales in that neighbourhood. From these numbers you can tell things like - if this area is popular with buyers, and if there's enough inventory turnover on a regular basis to make a good living.

3. The length of the commute to downtown.

4. The amount home values have increased over time compared to other areas nearby.

5. Is it the area where you live? This is an advantage because it makes your passion for the area more logical, but it's not necessary at all. It just makes

for a little less explaining if somebody asks where you live now.

Pick Your Specialization With The Google Keyword Planner

After you've narrowed your possible areas of specialization with the criteria above you go to the Google Keyword Planner. You need to set up a Google AdWords account to use the Keyword Planner, but you don't have to spend any money. In practical terms it just means you have to login to your Google account before you use the Keyword Planner. This is a screenshot of the first page you'll see when you login into the Google Keyword Planner.

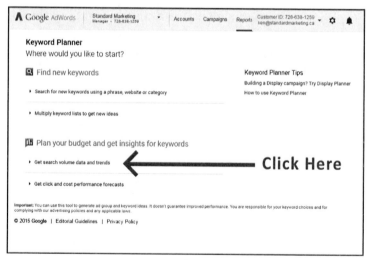

Make a list of all the possible phrases to do with real estate for each area you are considering, and input them into the area under "Option 1: Enter Keywords".

Here is the list of keyword phrases we use. You can add or delete phrases as you wish. And of course each time you do this search for a different area you insert the area you're looking at in the brackets. But don't include the brackets.

(your area) real estate	real estate for sale (your area)
(your area) real estate for sale	real estate agent (your area)
(your area) real estate agent	real estate agents (your area)
(your area) real estate agents	real estate agent (your area)
(your area) realtor	real estate agents (your area)
(your area) realtors	realtor (your area)
(your area) realty	realtors (your area)
(your area) homes for sale	realty (your area)
(your area) condos for sale	homes for sale (your area)
(your area) townhouse for sale	condos for sale (your area)
(your area) townhouses for sale	townhouse for sale (your area)
(your area) townhome for sale	townhouses for sale (your area)
(your area) townhomes for sale	townhome for sale (your area)
(your area) farm for sale	townhomes for sale (your area)
(your area) farms for sale	farm for sale (your area)
(your area) lot for sale	farms for sale (your area)
(your area) lots for sale	lot for sale (your area)
(your area) property for sale	lots for sale (your area)
(your area) properties for sale	property for sale (your area)
(your area) acreage for sale	properties for sale (your area)
(your area) acreages for sale	acreage for sale (your area)
(your area) open houses	acreages for sale (your area)
real estate (your area)	open houses (your area)

I copy my list of real estate related keyword phrases into a small Windows program called "Notepad". You'll find Notepad by clicking the "Start" button in the bottom left corner of your computer Desktop. Then click "All Programs", then the folder called "Accessories". After my list is in Notepad I copy and paste it into the Keyword Planner.

When I want to search for a different area I click the "Modify Search" button on the Keyword Planner, go back to Notepad and click "Edit", "Replace". I insert the name of the old area in the top field, the name of the next area I want to examine into the bottom field, and click "Replace All". Then I copy and paste that list from Notepad into the Keyword Planner again.

I choose an area that has 1,000 to 1,500 people searching for it on average per month for all keyword phrases combined. That means I only have to look at the blue bar graphs.

You can see a screenshot video of me with voice-over, doing this process on this page on the Top Agent Internet Marketing Website – http://www.topagentinternetmarketing.com/SOLD/specialization/

Then you optimize your website for the area you chose. Your main keyword phrase should be either "(your area) real estate" or "(your area) real estate for sale", whichever phrase has more people searching for it.

N. Why Page One of Google Is Not Enough

Why should you look for the smallest region that has enough prospects searching for it? Because the smaller the area the easier it is to get your website to the top of the Google search results page, and the faster everything will happen.

Did you catch that? We're not talking about getting your website on page one of the search results. We're talking about getting your website to the TOP of page one of the search results. It's an absolute necessity. Why?

Internet usage has changed drastically even in the last few years. One of the changes is that Google has become so good at showing search results of websites with the answers people are looking for, that 85% of people just click one of the top three websites in the organic search results.

Hardly anybody goes to page 2 or 3 anymore, or even scrolls down page 1. Different surveys show different numbers. After studying the credible surveys we tell our clients that on average:

    a. 35 to 45% of all people who search for anything on Google click only the first website in the search results.

    b. 20 to 25% of all people who search on Google click only the second website in the search results.

    c. 10 to 12% of people who use Google click the only the third website in the search results.

You can see that the number goes down very quickly. Each time you go down one spot you lose about half the traffic to your website.

The unfortunate part of this situation is that there's so many websites ranking in the bottom half of page one of Google, not getting any traffic to their website and they don't know why. This is why.

You can see a short screenshot video with voice-over of me explaining more about this point on the Top Agent Internet Marketing website – http://www.topagentinternetmarketing.com/SOLD/top3spots.

O. How Specialization Can Work for Brokers

It's sometimes a challenge finding a specialization for brokerages because some of them want to cover a very large area.

However, even if the broker won't specialize in one small area there are steps we can take to ameliorate the situation. We can include content for many areas on their website but put "nofollow" Meta Tags on all areas but one. The "nofollow" tags make it so Google will ignore those pages when calculating the website's rankings. This way the broker's website can rank well for one area, but still have content for all areas.

Conclusion

In this chapter we learned that although most people use the internet to search for real estate most real estate agents are not using the internet well. If you do, you'll have an unfair advantage over your competition.

We learned how Google works, their ranking criteria for both the regular organic listings and for Google My Business listings. We learned Google's most important ranking criteria is relevance. We learned why Specialization will bring you more prospects and leads than you've ever had before, and how to pick the best area to specialize in.

We learned why you need to be at the top of page one of Google, not just somewhere on page one. And we learned how Specialization can be good for brokers as well as for individual agents.

Chapter 3 talks about some of the challenges being a real estate agent and what to do about them. I also recount a marvelous conversation I had with a top agent about the attitude she used to get to the top and stay there.

JOIN OUR FREE WEBINAR AS A COMPANION TO THIS BOOK –

★ Register Now due to limited number of participants – Go to http://www.topagentinternetmarketing.com/ FreeWebinar

"How Top Real Estate Agents are Using the Internet to Capture More Leads and Close More Sales"

- See more Real Life Examples

- Learn Advanced Strategies

- Watch the actual concepts and processes described in this book done for you live

- Qualify for a Free One-on-One Consultation ($500 value)

- Enter your name for a Free Website Analysis ($1,200 value)

CHAPTER 3
THE BEST JOB IN THE WORLD
IF YOU DO IT RIGHT

© Randy Glasbergen
glasbergen.com

GLASBERGEN

"You're right, I owe all my success to luck! I'm lucky that my alarm clock
rings at 5:00 so I can get to work before everyone else. I'm lucky that
my car has a CD player so I can listen to self-improvement programs while
I commute. I'm lucky there are electric lights in my office so I can stay late...."

Real estate sales can be the best job in the world. We all know top agents like that.

Some are very hard working. And some work when they want and take long holidays to major events in exotic places around the world. They combine their travels with contributions to worthwhile causes in third world countries, which they publicize in a third party way so they don't look like they're bragging. And they get involved with local charities so they're seen as an important part of the community. It's just good marketing.

Everyone wants to know the secrets of their success.

Brokers court them. News reporters seek out their opinion on real estate issues. On top of everything else they get to help a lot of nice people find the home of their dreams, or profit from a tremendous investment.

They handle the most crucial parts of every deal. But in some ways they don't really do real estate sales anymore. They have become "marketers" for their multi-million dollar personal real estate corporation. I don't mean that's bad. That's very good. That's the way to make money in any business.

Some people will say top agents have just been lucky, but the truth is they've done many things right for a long time. If you do it right the rewards in real estate sales can be truly outstanding.

A. Are You Doing It Right?

If you don't know how to do it right real estate sales can be tough.

The whole business is based on referrals but how do you get referrals? One person can only have so many good friends. Will they all remember you years from now when somebody asks them if they know a good real estate agent? How do you make referrals like that happen?

And even if you make them happen somehow down the road, what do you live on until then?

How do you find people who are interested in doing business now? And what about next month, and the month after that? Do you have to ride the roller coaster, boom and bust, feast and famine, never knowing how much money you're going to make from one month to the next?

Part of the problem is that so many people are getting into the business. They are yearning for the freedom of being their own boss, making their own working hours, having no limit to their income.

The Association of Real Estate License Law Officials (ARELLO) estimates there are two million active real estate licensees in the United States alone. You don't need a university degree or even special training. In most of the US and Canada any 18 year old with high school graduation can become a fully licenced, legally accredited real estate agent.

And unless you work for a 100% house your startup costs are almost nothing.

B. What's Different About You?

With so much competition out there what are you doing to differentiate yourself? The challenge is to figure out a compelling reason why complete strangers should choose you over any other agent. Are you smarter, more experienced, more charming, or have a better looking marketing plan?

Some agents will say that they're branding themselves with a logo and a special look to their marketing materials. Of course that's good but if that's all you're doing you are headed for disappointment and failure.

The strangest thing about real estate sales is that many people get into it without realizing it's a people business. The properties, the rules and regulations, the sales techniques are all details. They're important, but they're details. The crucial ability you need is to be able to meet and talk to people.

I was surprised when I first heard that most agents don't answer their phones or return their phone calls. Then I kept hearing about someone who had to call four or five agents before one of them called back. Are these the same agents who are going to charm two or three total strangers every month into letting them sell their home?

When you meet someone do you know what to say so they like you and find you interesting? How do you ask for their contact information? And after you meet them do you take full advantage of what you've learned about them or is it wasted, along with all the time and money you invested in meeting them?

The question is, are you continually building your business, or starting every day over again from scratch?

Even if you're making a decent living you can be working so much you don't have any family time. You miss your daughter's school concerts and your son's playoff games. Your wife used to complain you were never at home until she started having coffee every night with her friends. What can they be talking about every night?

You go to a lot of networking events to meet new people even though talking to strangers makes you nervous. You stop off for a quick drink afterwards to calm your nerves, and tell yourself you do it only because you like it. You can quit any time you want. Once in a while you actually meet somebody who says they might be interested in selling their home, but most of the time it turns out to be a lot of hard work for nothing.

When you do get a listing there's so much work that goes with it you have trouble getting it all done. But you can't afford to hire an assistant. And so many people want you to cut your commission. They have no idea the amount of work involved. Pretty soon you feel like you're working for nothing. What's the use of it all? This isn't why you got into real estate.

When you're between deals you feel a heaviness in the

middle of your chest, and low-grade desperation in your voice. You get a little too excited and talk a bit too loud at inappropriate times, but you just smile and look away and hope nobody notices. What else can you do?

And even though you haven't had a real holiday in three years you don't dare take one now. If you're not out there beating the bushes nothing is happening. Heaven help you if you got sick or were in a car accident. At times like this you think you should have been a bus driver. They make good enough money, have a steady pay-check, no pressure, health insurance, and holidays every year.

So although top agents live a very good life, for many real estate agents life is tougher. But why? It really doesn't have to be. I'll never forget reading an Ogopogo comic in the newspaper at the kitchen table many years ago when I was a kid. Ogopogo said "We have met the enemy and he is us".

C. Creating Your Life The Way You Want

One of my business mentors was speaking at an event a few weeks ago. He said that whatever level of success you have in your life right now is the amount you can handle right now. To create more wealth and abundance you have to grow as a person.

He said the first step in creating a better life is to take full responsibility for everything in your life. It doesn't mean all the crap in your life is your fault. It's about you dealing with and managing the people and events in your life so that in the end things turn out the way you want them to.

He said people who believe their success is dependent on forces beyond their control will always find excuses why things don't work out, instead of doing whatever it takes to make them work out. He said successful people take full responsibility for everything in their lives, even their health.

This was an eye-opener for me. So I'm fully responsible for my own success? Well then, what do I have to do?

D. Almost Everybody Has Some Fear of Success

How do I know almost everybody has some fear of success? Because people resist change. It's in our nature to resist change. To be more successful would be a major change. That's unknown territory. What would I do? Would I make a mistake and look foolish in front of important people?

Over the years I've seen a lot of resistance to change in real estate agents. Some resist technology. Some resist letting go of the reins, hiring an assistant to do part of the work.

Some resist learning about marketing because they think it's not necessary. If you're thinking like that let me ask you this – do you think the top agent with $2,000,000 income every year started thinking about marketing after she was making that much money, or before?

Some agents resist investing in marketing their business because they don't know how to do it wisely. That's understandable. Some resist using systems because they think it will restrict their freedom or that it's too much work. I guess that's understandable too but it's really a crying shame. They're making their life so much harder than it has to be.

The truth is that having a system and working the system will give them more free time than they've ever had before. One of the biggest secrets to success in any business is to set up systems, and the same is true in real estate sales. You'll know a good system when you see it because it's simple to set up, simple to use, and it makes some part of your business run automatically.

I completely understand if you're one of those agents who resists technology. I didn't even get a computer until 10 years after most other people did. I was determined not to. There's too many things to learn these days - too many choices at the coffee shop, too many cards in my wallet, and now, too many computer programs to learn.

I resisted change until I figured out that all those choices meant there was something just right for me already available, and all I had to do was find it. That's better than what I want not being available. So I started investing the time to do a little research and find something just right for me.

Now I love going to the coffee shop because I get exactly what I want and it's delicious. Most of my cards are at home in a drawer and I have only three in my wallet. And I have a computer that almost never causes me problems (knock on wood), and I use it every day of my life. I love it. I can do so many things in seconds that used to take me hours or even days.

Something I've learned is that in order to be really successful in business I need to take some time each week to step back and work "on" my business, instead of working "in" my business. I believe the same is true in any business. Setting aside a little time to research and learn new things leads to freedom.

If you figure out what parts of your job an assistant can do, you can hire and train somebody to do those parts. If you don't have a database for your contacts we highly recommend you look into CRM software and spend whatever time it takes to input new information into it every day. It will help you make more money, and become more valuable to you than you ever thought possible.

If you want a steady stream of prospects contacting you every month you could learn something about internet marketing, and research which is the right internet marketing firm for you. Perhaps you're already doing that.

E. A Top Agent Talks About Personal Success

I like working with sales people as clients because almost all of them are very nice people. It's harder to be successful if you're not. I bumped into one of our top agent clients, Jenny, at a conference one time few years ago and asked her how she always manages to be happy and friendly.

To my surprise she stopped in her tracks and looked me in the eye for a moment to see if I was serious, then waved me over to a table and we sat down. She told me she wasn't always this way. She spent her early years being very unhappy, with low self-esteem.

It's always interesting for me to hear that a very happy person has been very unhappy in their past. It makes me wonder if perhaps the one is based on the other. Anyway, Jenny said in her early twenties she was looking for ways to improve her life and read a self-help book that said "Life is for learning."

1. How to Make No Failures, No Mistakes

When she read that she decided that from now on she wasn't going to make mistakes or have failures. They were all just "learning experiences". When something goes wrong she doesn't take it personally. She doesn't say "Why me? What did I do to deserve this?" like she used to. It's a learning experience. She looks at the situation to see if there's anything she can learn, and keeps on going.

That small shift in thinking helped her change her attitude toward herself and her life from negative to positive, and her career started to take off.

I wasn't expecting such a meaningful answer to my question, but Jenny kept on going.

2. **Avoiding Drama**

She said another thing that helped was something her mother told her. Her mother was an intelligent lady, but an alcoholic. In one of her lucid moments she told Jenny she should always be a little detached from people, even her loved ones. Most people create unnecessary drama in their lives, and they try to draw you into their drama to validate it, to prove that it's real and that their lives are important.

But as soon as you get drawn in, she said, you're lost. You're a bit player in someone else's fantasy, and it only creates problems for yourself and others.

In order not to lose yourself you need to be a little bit detached. You can still love someone and be detached from what they're doing and saying. In fact, when you're detached you can give them the kind of support they really need, perhaps a hug, or just someone to listen.

At the end of that short conversation her mother encouraged her to watch out for when Jenny was creating her own unnecessary drama. She said most of the problems in our lives we create ourselves and they're completely unnecessary.

Jenny paused, and said she hadn't really intended to talk so much, but her daughter had asked her this same question recently about how she could be happy almost all of the time, and she'd been thinking about what she was going to say to her. Did I want to hear more? I said I was really interested in what she had to say. So she continued.

3. Happiness Is A Choice

Jenny told me her grandmother was a very special person. She only saw her upset once when Jenny was about 12 years old. Her grandmother had great raspberry bushes in her garden and was standing at the stove making jam but something had gone wrong. A number of jars had been ruined.

Her grandmother swore, which was very unusual, and Jenny could see her face turn bright red. Then she said to herself something like, "Oh, I'm not going to let that ruin my grandchildren's visit, took a deep breath and smiled, and came back to the kitchen table to their game of canasta. She was completely cheerful!

Jenny didn't realize it at the time but that small incident had a big impact on her. From then on, whenever something made her upset she thought of her grandma at the stove, took a deep breath, and changed her mood back to being happy. After a while she realized she could do that anytime she wanted. She didn't think much of it until she noticed other people hanging on to bad moods for days at a time. What a shame.

4. I Like This Person

Then she said that when she meets a new person she thinks to herself, "I like this person". She said it's very strange, sometimes it's like they can hear her thought. They smile or lift their head a bit and look at her. And she thinks to herself, "I wonder what makes them special", and "How can I help them accomplish what's really important to them?"

Thinking those thoughts help her ask questions that get people talking about the most important issues in their lives. It helps them remember her. It gives her something meaningful to talk to them about the next time they meet. And if she ever really does anything meaningful to help them with their most important goals they are friends for life.

5. The Mysterious Power of Gratitude

Then she talked about gratitude. She said she heard Tony Robbins talk one time and he led them through a 10 minute gratitude visualization that had a strong impact on her. She felt so good after those few minutes that she committed to do it every morning from then on.

She's not sure why gratitude is so powerful. It seems to push all the negative feelings and energy that were building up inside her, out of her body or out of her thoughts. She feels fresh and optimistic that more things will come into her life that she can be grateful for.

6. Always Be Watching

Then she said she realized long ago that the only

constant in life is change. So when things are going
well she tries to be as watchful and careful as she is
when things are not going so well. It helps her to
be more constant, more consistent. She doesn't get
too excited when things seems to be going really
well, and doesn't get too upset when things seem to
be going badly.

7. **Long Term Vision**
The last thing she said was that she carries a vivid
picture of herself in her mind being very happy,
surrounded by her family and friends and everything she could possibly want. She even wrote it
all down on a piece of paper she keeps in a private
place at home. She believes it will come true, so it
helps her to remember that image when things are
not going as well as she'd like.

We had to get back to what was going on at the
conference, so I thanked her, and finished jotting
down some notes I was making while she talked.
Wow. That was a conversation I'll remember for
the rest of my life.

F. Real Estate Sales Is A Great Business
The last thing I want to say in this chapter is to encourage you not to lose faith in the real estate sales business.
Although it can be tough the opportunities for wealth and
freedom are still there. Actually, in some ways the business
is easier than it's ever been.

The opportunities opened up by the internet are tremendous. You just have to know where to find them. It's
not even that hard if you know what you're looking for.

And they're not just available to tech savvy computer geeks. They're available to anybody. You just need to be careful who you deal with. Internet Marketing companies are the same as any industry whether you're talking about doctors, lawyers, or Indian Chiefs – some are very good, some are very bad, and most are somewhere in between.

The annual report issued by the National Association of Realtors® on November 3, 2014 found that 92% of buyers searched for their home on the internet. It also found that buyers who used the Internet were more likely to purchase their home through an agent than those who didn't.

The internet can be a reliable method of bringing in large numbers of prospects on a regular, steady, monthly basis. In this book we will help you become aware of the most common problems with internet marketing and how to avoid them. Then we will show you how to uncover the opportunities and give you step-by-step instructions on how to take full advantage of them.

As you've already seen, although the internet is the main focus of this book it does not deal exclusively with internet issues. We want to add value to your life and your career in any way we can.

Sometimes it's easy to forget that top agents didn't start at the top. They started at the bottom just like you did. Anybody can be at top agent with the right attitude, the right information, and the right action.

The backbone of any career in real estate is referrals. Good internet marketing can supercharge your real estate career by bringing large numbers of prospects to your website and getting them to trust you enough to call and arrange a meeting.

After that you can take over. Your friendliness, humility, professionalism, and focus on their needs will turn them into a happy client, a source of sales and referrals for years to come.

Conclusion

In this chapter we talked about real estate sales at its best, and at its worst. We talked a bit about personal responsibility and I shared my conversation with a top agent about how she manages to be happy and productive almost all the time.

And we talked about how the new opportunities brought by the internet can be an easy-to-use system that automatically brings in prospects every month on a regular basis.

The next chapter looks specifically at five common myths that can really hurt your success if you're not careful, and talks about how to avoid them.

CHAPTER 4
FIVE MYTHS AND THE TRUTH
THAT WILL SET YOU FREE

© 2001 Randy Glasbergen.
www.glasbergen.com

"Welcome to the Weight Loss Forum.
To lose one pound, double-click
your mouse six million times."

There are myths about weight loss, about real estate sales, and about internet marketing. When I look at my past I realize that myths are what I reached for when I was hoping things would be different than they actually were. And when things didn't turn out as I hoped, when something I tried didn't work, myths were a justification that most of my friends would believe, for why I didn't accomplish my goal.

When I didn't feel like solving my own problems, or I didn't feel capable, when it was easier to blame something outside myself for my lack of success, invoking a popular myth was easier than taking charge of my life, being totally responsible for my success or failure.

But then one day I decided to start creating my life the way I wanted it to be. That was a hard day, and a good day. It was hard because it meant I had to accept responsibility for all the things in my life that I didn't like. It was good day because I felt like I was free for the first time, free of the judgements and burdens and the blame. I was free to bring anything I wanted into my life.

Since then my life has been much more successful and happy, and I've enjoyed exposing myths, bringing the hard truth of reality to light. I say "hard truth" because life is hard. I don't think there's any way around that. All I can do is not make it harder than it already is.

Believing in myths makes my life harder because it means I'm not making decisions based on accurate information. I'm avoiding the truth. To be successful I have to be willing to look into the situation and find out what's right for me. I need to be open to learning new things and taking positive action.

Have a look at the myths below that I've come across dealing with real estate agents for many years, and the real world truths that will set you free.

Myth #1 - Word of Mouth is All I Need to Get Referrals

Many agents that I talk to, when I ask them "What are you doing to get referrals? What drives your business right now?" They say "Well, you know, most of my business is coming from word of mouth".

I say, "You mean, hope".

Most struggling agents hope to get word of mouth,

hope to get referrals, hope prospects will show up, and hope that when clients want to sell their home again, or know somebody who wants to sell their home, they'll call them.

But "Hope" is not a strategy.

It's important to understand that there is "Active" word of mouth, and "Passive" word of mouth.

In "Active word of mouth" you are constantly doing things to stay in touch, positioning yourself as a trusted advisor, putting yourself in front of your sphere of influence constantly to remind them you're there to help, to serve them.

With Active word of mouth they can't possibly forget you. They like you. So when the time comes and they can give something back in return for all you've done for them, they call you. Successful agents understand that word of mouth doesn't mean doing nothing, hoping that referrals and prospects shows up.

Let me give you an example.

Tony has been a friend of mine since we were kids. We had some wild times in high school but drifted apart when I left town. He's been in real estate sales now for about eight years and is very successful. One evening over a quiet drink he told me that he almost left the real estate business after only a few months. He told me this story.

He remembers getting out of bed one morning while the house was still dark and everyone was asleep, just standing, looking out the bedroom window for the longest time really dreading the thought of going to work that day. He saw a man walking down the street and wished quietly that he was that man and had his life instead of his own.

He would remember that moment for the rest of his life. What an unhappy time.

Tony was 37 years old, his wife didn't spend a lot of money, and she followed him wherever he said they needed to go for his work. But she was becoming more distant as the years went by and he continued to make less money. He had a mortgage and credit card debt up to his eyeballs. He was using some of his credit cards to pay the minimum payments on his other credit cards.

A few years ago his wife's parents lent them $30,000 that they'd used to pay off their credit cards, but somehow they had huge debts again already. After a few years her parents realized they weren't going to get their money back so they said they'd reduce her share of their estate in their will by that amount.

Tony went into real estate sales because he felt he was unemployable. Every boss he'd ever had was an idiot. Why was that? Surely all bosses weren't idiots. He always tried to help them by pointing out when they'd made a mistake. He desperately tried to do a good job, but for one reason or another something always seemed to happen and they had to let him go.

If it wasn't for his wife's job he didn't know what they would do. But they needed more than that to get by. A few years earlier he'd talked an old friend into giving him a job as his marketing manager. So for about three years there between him and his wife they were making over a $100,000 a year, but they were still broke. He honestly didn't know why. It didn't seem that expensive to hire a magician for their son's birthday party. Didn't everybody do that?

Anyway, somehow he'd screwed up that job too. He didn't even know what he'd done wrong. His friend just told him one day they were restructuring the company. And there was nothing he could do.

He didn't really want to leave the kids, actually. And his wife used to respect him when he was providing well for the family, so maybe she would respect him again if he was successful. He felt this was the end of the line. He had to make this job work.

He started his career by taking every training course he could find. Later he realized that he took all those training courses so he wouldn't have to actually talk to somebody. He hated the idea of pushing himself on people. Nobody wanted to talk to a pushy salesman. If people wanted to find out about a property they could call him.

He felt awkward talking to strangers. **He'd never been good at small talk.** He hated networking events that didn't have a schedule where you always had something to do. And the last thing in the world he was going to do, was go door to door and have people slam the door in his face.

He'd been lucky and sold a five bedroom house to a friend of his father's after only three months. But if he didn't do another deal soon he wasn't sure what he was going to do. He was desperate. He kept phoning the same people over and over again hoping for another referral. But they were starting to get tired of it.

Tony and I bumped into each other in the old neighbourhood one Sunday afternoon when I was visiting my mother. I'd been back to town for a while but didn't look him up because I had problems of my own. And he didn't tell me the truth about his situation because he was too embarrassed.

When I told him what I was doing, that I had a successful company bringing prospects and leads to real estate agents through their website he jumped at it. Investing in internet marketing seemed about the same to him as investing in training courses, and he wouldn't have to knock on doors.

We built him a website, chose a good neighbourhood for him to specialize in, and that started him off. After a few months leads were coming to him. He made some deals, started keeping a good database, volunteered in the neighbourhood, and was encouraged by his success. **He told me it became easier to talk to people when he had steady money coming in.** He started to feel like an expert, and his business grew. That was over eight years ago. Now he's not only getting referrals from his website clients, but also from friends and acquaintances. He takes six weeks holiday with his wife in a different country every year, and their relationship has never been better.

He tells everybody he owes his success to me, and although I appreciate the compliment it's not really true. He's the one who made the right decisions at the right times, and did the actual work. Nothing would have happened if he hadn't been writing up offers and closing deals.

Tony's story exposes the myth that all you need is word of mouth to get referrals. It demonstrates one of the real world truths about the real estate business these days – that it's very difficult to build a successful career if you don't have a reliable steady stream of new prospects coming in every month.

Of course you need a database. You need to add as many people as you can to it, and provide them with either interesting or valuable information to keep yourself top of mind. Your website and internet marketing can start you off and take your career in real estate sales as far as you want it to go.

Myth #2 - Internet Marketing is Too Expensive

Here's another popular myth about being a real estate agent. I met Stan at a presentation I was doing in

Richmond, which is a bedroom community of Vancouver. He came up afterwards and asked me some questions. He's a friendly guy so I was happy to talk to him. After that he would call me every once in a while with a question about social media, and we had some good talks but nothing ever came of it.

He's middle aged, almost what you would call "a senior", and has been in real estate sales for 5 years. He knows a lot of people so he's managed to do four or five ends a year from people he meets around town, at his golf club, and from leads he gets from small ads in the local real estate newspaper. In Richmond an end is worth $9,800. His wife works so they manage to get by. We all know agents like Stan.

He has no database or even a spreadsheet with information on past clients. He writes down things about people he meets on napkins and little pieces of paper and puts them in a drawer in his desk. But doesn't do anything with them. He doesn't contact them by email, postal mail, or even by phone. He relies on bumping into them around the neighbourhood or on the golf course.

Even though the market is doing well Stan's sales have been dropping and he doesn't know what to do. He has a $50 a month website from a template company but doesn't write blogs or put up testimonials, and won't spend any money on Internet Marketing. He keeps asking me questions about social media because he sees it as a way he can bring in prospects without spending any money. But it hasn't been working.

Now compare Stan's story with Lauren's. I use Lauren because she's in the same market as Stan. She's 28 years old. She was brand new to real estate when she came to us ten months ago. She's not what you'd call glamourous but is always clean and neat, and she does it without having to wear a different outfit every day of the year. The best thing about her is her open and confident smile. She smiles a lot. I asked her one time over coffee if she'd always been so confident and happy, and how she managed to do it while starting a new career. She told me she fakes it. **She pretends to be confident and happy, and after a while it just comes naturally.** When I heard that I knew this gal was going to go far.

She also had a $50 website from a template company, but knew that people search on the internet for real estate so she was determined to get to the top of Google. Our minimum was a lot for somebody starting out but she bit the bullet and went for it because she knew it was important.

We picked out a neighbourhood she knew and liked for her to specialize in, one that had a good amount of people searching for it every month. We fixed up her website, and started working on her rankings. She was already on a softball team. She joined a Lions Club in her neighborhood, started volunteering, and finds out as much as she can about everybody she meets. **She says it's easy to find out interesting things about people. She just asks them questions about themselves. Almost everybody likes to talk about them self.** And she puts it all into her CRM.

It took four months before she got a good lead from her website, and five months before she closed a deal from one of her personal connections. But since then she's been getting an increasing number of calls from her website every month. And she's closing deals both from her personal connections and from prospects who contacted her from her website.

Lauren is a very common sense business person. She'll tell you that anything is too expensive if it doesn't bring a good return. Then no matter how cheap it is, it costs too much.

Her story exposes the myth that Internet Marketing is too expensive, and brings to light the real world truth that if it brings a satisfactory return then, within reason, it doesn't matter what it costs. Then it's a paying investment.

And if you look at it as an investment, all you need to do is invest wisely with the right firm. Chapter 10 will help you choose right firm.

Myth #3 - You Don't Need To Spend Money To Make Money

Lauren's story also explodes the myth that you don't have to spend money to make money. She is well on her way to reaching her goal of $70,000 in her first year, and we feel she'll make twice that in her second year. Even with all her hard work it would be very difficult for her to have such a good start to her career if she wasn't spending money on internet marketing.

While it's true that a few agents have built a solid career just with referrals, my feeling is that it takes a very special type of person to do that. I heard one real estate trainer say you have to call up every person you've ever known, people you went to high school with, long lost relatives, everyone, and tell them you're in real estate.

Now, I'm good with people. I'm confident, sincere, and genuinely try to help them. But I don't think I could do that. And I'm not sure I know anybody who could do that and make it work well. So if you're like me, if you're one of the many and don't mind admitting it, then internet marketing can be a very easy way to bring in lots of qualified prospects on a reliable basis.

Of course the old timers in the real estate business built their careers just with referrals. They had to because there wasn't any internet. And they worked hard at it for a long time. The cost of living was lower then. You could support yourself for less while you were waiting for referrals to come in.

Another change since the old days is that home prices have skyrocketed. And most people getting into real estate sales are young like Lauren. The United States Census **2011 American Housing Survey** shows that the typical homeowner is 54 years old. (source – realtor.org) Lauren's friends can't afford today's high prices. She needs an additional source of leads other than her friends. She's using both internet marketing and referrals.

The truth about the myth that you don't have to spend money to make money is that it's out of date. These days you must spend money to make money. The only alternative is to support yourself for many years while your circle of influence is growing. But even if you do that you'll still be spending money on living expenses and operating expenses for a long time, and you'll be broke for a long time.

This is a very general myth. Of course we wouldn't recommend charging out the door and just spending money on anything. We recommend educating yourself in marketing, and in internet marketing. We feel that if you do that, you'll see you can supercharge your career with internet marketing and start living in abundance years ahead of those who don't.

Myth #4 - I Don't Need Internet Marketing if I Have a Website

Being around real estate agents for many years I've heard this myth a number of times. If you're one of those agents please understand that I'm not trying to make you wrong. I'd just like to tell you what some agents say when they call and ask about our services.

Actually, because we've been in business for 16 years most of our business comes from referrals. The first time a real estate agent calls, the conversation starts out something like this:

"Hey Ken, My name is John. I was referred to you by …………… They said you guys are good at Internet Marketing. I've had my website for about three years and I've never got a thing from it. Can you help me with that?"

I say, "Hey John. So tell me, what kind of help are you looking for?"

John, "Well, I need more traffic to my website. I've spent hours writing my bio, putting my open houses and new listings on my blog, and adding testimonials. I even did a video and put it on my website, but it hasn't helped at all. I've spent countless hours on Facebook adding photos and information but I must be doing it wrong because nothing is coming in."

The above is a very common conversation in our office. The National Association of Realtors says 76% of their members have a website. From my experience I would estimate that 80% of those get absolutely nothing from it. It's an online brochure.

The only people who find it are people that they've given their business card to, that they've emailed with their website in their email signature, or that are searching for them by name on Google.

Having a website and not doing Internet Marketing is like buying a new car and never taking it out of your garage, like buying a new evening gown and never wearing it. Nobody will ever see it. It's a waste.

If you pick a good area to specialize in, if you add lots of valuable text and information about your area to your website, if you set all the technical things up properly, set up your social media accounts well, write good blogs, and build high quality backlinks, in short, if you show Google your website is an authority in your area with content that is always up-to-date, Google will give you high rankings.

You'll get hundreds of actively searching prospects to your website every month who are looking for an expert in your area, to help them either sell their home or buy one in your area.

The truth is that doing internet marketing on a regular monthly basis is an absolute must. Nobody will ever see your website if you don't.

Myth #5 - Specialization Will Hurt Your Business

This myth is very dangerous. It leads straight to wasted marketing dollars, failure and disappointment. But it's a little bit new because it's based on the internet, so we need to understand it.

Real estate agents looking into internet marketing for the first time sometimes tell me they want to be at the top of Google for the keyword phrase "(major market) real estate". Just insert the name of your city in the brackets. It could be any major market in the US or Canada.

I certainly don't blame them. They would definitely get a lot of leads from their website. What they don't understand is that there are probably 40,000 people every month searching on Google for that phrase. As we discussed in Chapter 2, if their website is Number 1 they're going to get 20,000 prospects to their website every month.

That's how much traffic the Number 1 website for that phrase in your market is getting right now, roughly. I hope you can see that we're talking about a different league than an individual real estate agent's website. It's only major directories and long established national brand brokerages that have deep enough pockets to be Number 1 on Google for very general phrases like that.

It would take an Internet Marketing budget of $30,000 a month for three years to bump one of those companies out of that top spot on Google. On top of that you'd have to build a real estate directory website that focused only on your market. Most people don't understand that rankings on Google are like the Richter scale. The closer you get to the top, the harder it is to move up. When you get into the big leagues, it's very hard.

This means that the only possible way to get noticed is to be a big fish in a small pond. To get any traffic at all to your website you have to specialize. To help our clients understand the situation we ask them **"Would you rather have a piece of a small pie, or no pie at all?"**

But there's no need to be discouraged. There are great opportunities in specialization and a great deal of money to be made. You just have to be good at picking your battles, of course I mean your area of specialization. Sometimes that specialization could be as small as a single neighbourhood, and still have enough prospects searching for it every month to make you a great deal of money.

To get you high rankings we have to show Google your website is an authority in that neighbourhood, and to do that we need to make your website exclusively about that neighbourhood, as we discussed in Chapter 1.

An agent named Jordan called my office the other day. I was talking to him about Specialization, and he said, "But if my website talks only about that neighborhood I'm going to lose business from all the other neighborhoods".

I said, "Jordan, tell me honestly now, how much business are you getting from your website from those other neighborhoods right now."

"None, actually. I've never gotten anything from my website."

"I admire your honesty," I said. "Thank you. It's the same for most of the agents who call us. We recommend Specializing in one neighborhood because that's the way to get high rankings on Google. When you've got high rankings you get hundreds of qualified prospects coming to your website every month, and many will be serious enough to contact you.

We put lots of high quality, valuable information about that neighborhood on your website, and write the text in a way that people can tell you love that neighborhood. When sellers see that, they want you to sell their home because you love the neighborhood as much as they do. They know you'll sell their home with passion.

When buyers see all that information about that neighborhood they see that you know everything there is to know about that neighborhood, and that you'll find them a home they're going to love."

Jordan, "OK, sounds good. But what about people who come to my website who live in other neighborhoods?"

Me, "Actually because we're not optimizing your website for those neighbourhoods you'll probably continue to get the same amount of traffic from those neighbourhoods as you are getting now."

Pause.

Jordan chuckles, "I see."

Me, "But of course over time, after you're doing lots of deals on a regular basis in the neighborhood you're specializing in, your clients will refer their family and friends who live in other parts of the city. And they'll be happy to deal with you on the strength of the referral, just because you're a real estate expert, and you did such a good job for their friend.

They won't care that you're a specialist in another neighborhood. They just want to deal with a good man."

So the myth that Specialization will hurt your business couldn't be farther from the truth. Specialization is an incredible marketing opportunity that the internet has made even more powerful than ever.

Conclusion

In this chapter we learned about why myths are popular, and about some of the most harmful ones with regard to Marketing and Internet Marketing. And we looked at some good examples to find the truth.

In the next chapter we'll talk about one of the most important concepts in marketing, Brand/Image advertising vs Direct Response advertising. After that we talk about the power of educating your clients, my personal story about how I became successful in Internet Marketing for real estate agents, and how to do Pay Per Click advertising profitably.

CHAPTER 5
BRANDING VS DIRECT RESPONSE

© Randy Glasbergen
glasbergen.com

GLASBERGEN

"No, your flood insurance doesn't pay if
you're flooded with junk mail and catalogs."

There are so many places you can spend your advertising budget. Let me ask you these questions:

- Are you sick and tired of wasting money on advertising that gets minimal results?

- Are you tired of riding the financial roller coaster, where sometimes you've got more appointments than you can handle, and other times you're alone and the world is a cold hard place?

- Have you ever wished you knew a proven, cost-effective marketing system that really worked, that produced a steady flow of new prospects consistently?

If you answered "YES" to one or more of these questions, then this chapter will open your eyes to what marketing and advertising are really all about.

A. What Advertising Sales Reps Don't Want You to Know

You often hear people say that for your real estate business to survive and thrive you need to get your name out there and build a brand so you can stand out among your competition.

WRONG!

In fact, brand-name recognition is just an over-hyped, over-priced lie that has led real estate agents just like you to waste hard-earned dollars on advertising concepts that don't work. It's one of the biggest mistakes I see real estate agents make. The point is that your ad doesn't need to get your name out there. Your ad needs to get your prospects to contact you.

"The sole purpose of marketing is to get more people to buy more of your product or your service, more often, for more money. That's the only reason to spend a single dime."

– Sergio Zyman, former chief marketing officer of Coca-Cola

All media reps, newspaper, bus benches, online sales, and yellow pages are highly persuasive on the topic of brand-name recognition or awareness. This is their bread-and-butter strategy, where they convince you that the reason you don't have enough listings is that no one knows you even exist.

Please understand this simple fact - advertising sales reps are paid based on how much business they bring in for their company. So the more money they get you to spend, the more money they make. Advertising sales reps are also keen to use the "frequency" and "repetition" cards as part of their persuasion strategy to get to you spend more money with them.

They often tell real estate agents that you need more exposure. And the way to get exposure is to keep running your ad, over and over again. The more often you run your ad, the more exposure you get. And people need to keep seeing your ad over and over again before they respond. They tell you to be patient. It's all about repetition.

No, it's not about repetition. It's about end results.

If your ad is ineffective, it doesn't matter how many times you repeat it. Think about it. If you're trying to reach someone but have the wrong phone number, will dialing the same number five more times make a difference? NO! It doesn't matter how many times you dial the number, you still won't get to the person you originally intended to reach.

Bottom line: Don't listen to sales reps' advice to repeat your ads (not even if they offer you a frequency discount) unless the ads are successful in bringing in new clients. Only repeat successful marketing campaigns − not the ones that flop!

A third sales tactic commonly used by media sales reps is the "bigger is better" strategy, that is, increase your ad size so your clients can notice you. If your ad isn't drawing enough attention from people, they say, it's because it's too small. They tell you to enlarge your ad size, so more people will notice it. They say, "Don't change the copy or ad design, just make the ad bigger!"

This thinking is ridiculous!

It's the same as a waiter saying, "Madam, you don't like the pie? Why don't you try a bigger piece?" Frequency and size sound like logical reasons for why people respond to advertising, but the truth is neither frequency nor ad size will make any difference if the ad doesn't work.

For example: in your daily commute, you drive by a restaurant twice a day – once on the way to work, and once on the way back. You obviously know this restaurant exists because you've seen its sign more than 1,000 times. But you have never once set foot in that restaurant, let alone eaten there.

This example clearly shows that brand name recognition has nothing to do with increasing sales. Brand-name recognition helps to confirm that your business exists, but it is insufficient to get serious prospects to contact you.

The most common problem in internet marketing, and in fact, in any kind of marketing and advertising is that business people don't understand how to bring direct results from their marketing spend, so they waste their budget on too much branding.

Don't get me wrong. Branding is good if you can make it happen at the same time as you're bringing in concrete leads. But Branding for its own sake is not the realm of small business. It's the realm of huge corporations with deep pockets who can afford to wait a long time to see results.

"Brand awareness is absolutely worthless unless it leads to sales."

B. How to Double or Triple Your Leads

Most real estate agents are really confused about what

marketing actually is. Many of them believe marketing is just doing some sort of advertising to promote themselves. You have to realize that advertising is just a small part of the process. Most real estate agents do not have a reliable, consistent new-prospect attraction system, nor do they know how to create one, let alone do any effective marketing at all.

And I don't blame them. Most real estate agents haven't had the training and simply don't have the tools to correctly attract prospects. Nor do they have the time to learn how to do the right things.

Maybe you have tried advertising in the newspaper, yellow pages, or on bus benches. Most likely, you were rarely successful. Why? Because it's not just where you advertise, but how you advertise that determines your results. Why does one type of advertising work for one real estate agent and not another? The reality is if you don't know how to use something, it probably won't work.

This is a good time to introduce you to Brand-Image Advertising vs Promotional Advertising. **All advertising can be broken down into two major categories: brand-image and promotional.**

The first type is commonly known as institutional advertising or branding. This is commonly taught in business schools and colleges. It is predominantly used by banks, insurance companies, and most big corporations. You've seen many examples of image advertising. It may have someone's logo or company name, maybe a clever slogan.

In their printed or online ads you can see that they use positive images of the company to convey key messages to its audience. It attempts to tell how great the company is, that it is trustworthy, reliable, and better than its competition. It attempts to give the company a look of professionalism. It attempts to make the prospects feel good about the company.

And the focus of brand-image advertising seems to be "me" advertising. Image ads perpetuate the false belief that if we look really good on the outside, then people are somehow going to be compelled to do business with us.

Think of your ad as an extra agent on your team. Would you hire another agent to get listings by contacting your prospects and just saying your name over and over - calling them on the phone, whispering your name, and hanging up?

You wouldn't send a member of your team to a stranger's home to hold up a sign with your name and logo and say, "Hi, We've been in business for 20 years. We have a pretty logo, look at us, aren't we great? Oh, you may have heard my name." You would expect a lot more than that from a salesperson on your team. Then why wouldn't you expect just as much from your ad as well?

Brand-image advertising makes sense for Kraft, Nike, and Sony. Huge companies have to spend money on that kind of advertising to keep their names out there in the commercial world. The idea is that when people make buying decisions, they will favor products whose names they know. And it works. Brand-name consumer products almost always outsell generic products.

Familiarity increases trust, and trust increases sales. The problem is, it is very, very expensive to create a household brand name. We are talking about tens of millions or even hundreds of millions of dollars.

Brand-building is for patient people with very deep

pockets. That's probably not us. So if you are a real estate agent working with a limited budget, we recommend you focus on response advertising. As mentioned earlier, if you develop brand recognition as a by-product, great. But do not spend money exclusively on creating it.

Promotional advertising, also known as response, or call-to-action advertising, is designed to get prospects to respond to your ad immediately, by picking up the phone or emailing you, so you can measure the results of your promotion.

Promotional advertising uses four main elements to engage prospects. In printed or online ads you can usually see:

1. An enticing offer.
2. How your product or service will improve their lives.
3. An explicit "call to action" with a sense of urgency, limited time or short supply.
4. A means of response such as a phone number, a website or specific webpage.

Unfortunately for most real estate agents the extent of their advertising efforts is nothing more than a enlarged version of their business card. Their ads typically have a picture of them, the logo of their brokerage, and a short slogan. "This is who I am, this is what I do, and here's my phone number."

Classic brand-image advertising.

There's a very high probability that prospective clients glancing over these real estate ads will not call and make an appointment. Why? Because prospective clients need to be given a reason to contact you.

A good ad should have a powerful benefit that captures the attention of your target audience. It overcomes objections, answers questions your prospects might have, it promises results, and makes a compelling offer for them to respond – now.

That reason could be that you are a specialist in your area, that you have some special information to give them, or that you're holding a free educational presentation. More about that later.

Keep in mind, an ad is going to cost you the same amount of money if you get one call or if you get 100 calls, so make your ad message count.

C. Four Important Rules of Promotional Advertising

Rule #1 - Never do anything that doesn't let you directly track its results.

Rule #2 - Never run an ad a second time if it didn't work the first time.

Rule #3 - Never fall in love with your ad.

Rule #4 - Never listen to anybody unless they can market better than you.

You may love an ad, you may think it's a winner; you may think it is the greatest ad you've ever designed. You run it, and it fails. Whether you're running Google AdWords, Facebook ads, newspaper ads, bus benches or direct mail, don't continue running it because you think it's great or because it's got your picture in it. Don't fall in love with your ad. Results rule. Period.

Opinions don't count. If an ad doesn't get prospects to call you, stop it. And one more thing: Time after time, I've seen a perfectly good ad being discarded because someone close to them said, Oh, I would never read that many words", or "That's not pretty enough." This is an important piece of advice: Don't listen to anyone who hasn't proven to you they can market their business better than you can.

It's better to just test the ad – let the results speak for themselves. Until you test your ad, anything that other people say is irrelevant, unless they are a proven marketer making lots of money in their real estate business.

Now that you fully understand the two types of advertising, and how advertising is just part of the marketing process, it's time to talk about what marketing is all about. Before I continue, let me first tell you …

D. What Real Marketing Is Not

Sometimes, knowing what NOT to do is as important as knowing what to do.

- Real Marketing is NOT getting your name out there.

- Real Marketing is NOT name recognition.

- Real Marketing is NOT building an image.

- Real Marketing is NOT getting your name in front of as many people as you can.

- Real Marketing is NOT bragging about how excellent you are.

- Real Marketing is NOT copying Fortune 500 companies' cute or funny marketing.

- Real Marketing is NOT cold-prospecting.

- Real Marketing is NOT begging people for referrals.

- Real Marketing is NOT going to networking meetings and social events to meet clients and prospects.

- Real Marketing is NOT having a brochure and business card. It's not even being good at what you do.

- Real Marketing is NOT winning an award. It's not having letters after your name.

- And finally, Real Marketing is NOT hoping and praying for prospects to call you. It's NOT pretending to have a predictable income stream from referrals only.

E. What Marketing Really Is

Real Marketing engages a diversified group of systems that automatically gets ideal prospects to contact you in a predictable manner. Ideal prospects are described as those who are pre-interested, pre-motivated, and pre-qualified. They will also happily refer their friends and family to you.

These systems run on autopilot and don't require active manual labor on your part. You don't want to be running around looking for prospective clients. You want to structure your marketing so that they automatically come to you.

With a Real Marketing system you will no longer have to worry where you next client will come from. You no longer have to worry about keeping your team busy. And you no longer have to worry about covering desk fees, E & O Insurance, and other recurring expenses. That is what a Real Marketing system can do for you.

Ask yourself:

- Do you know the lifetime value of your existing clients? Yes or No

- Do you know how much it costs to acquire a new client? Yes or No

- Do you have a marketing system in place to attract new prospects? Yes or No

- Do you know where your best clients come from? Yes or No

- Do you have trackable marketing systems in place? Yes or No

- Do you know what your return on investment is for every marketing dollar you spend? Yes or No

- Is your marketing a one dimensional approach or is it a system: multifaceted, strategic, incorporating online and offline combinations? Yes or No

If you answered "No" to these questions, you're guaranteed to be disappointed with your marketing results.

A good marketing system for your real estate business will do these things automatically 24 hours a day seven days a week:

A. Before they are your client:
1. Get you high rankings on Google so qualified prospects come to your website.
2. Your website shows them clearly you are the only agent they should deal with, and makes it so they contact you.

B. After they are your client:

1. Encourages them to give you a testimonial.
2. Encourages them to refer their relatives and friends.
3. Sends them continued value on an ongoing basis to keep you top of mind as their preferred real estate agent.

F. The Quickest, Easiest and Best Way to Get a Never Ending Supply of Prospects

Ask yourself: When prospective clients look for a real estate agent, how do they go about finding one? Where do they turn?

Common answers to this question are:

- Direct mail pieces they received today

- Their fridge magnets or calendars from agents

- Business cards from agents they met at recent networking events

While it's true that these are all methods of finding real estate agents, there is one place where more and more potential clients are searching for information on real estate: the Internet.

In fact, the growth of online search methods is showing constant signs of increasing! In fact, it's safe to say that for prospects under the age of 50 today...

If they can't find you online, you don't exist.

So when your prospects go searching, will they find you? Or are you like most other real estate agents, lost on the web? Or worst yet, would they find your competition before they find you? The Internet is the most reliable, predictable and consistent way of bringing in new, quality prospects. Love it or hate it, you need to stay on top of the expanding digital economy if you want a thriving real estate business.

Many of the real estate agents I talk to tell me about the pain and frustration they've had over the past few years trying to make their online marketing efforts work. Many also complain how costly it's been. Some have paid huge amounts of money, much of it wasted on a poor-performing website that gets them no clients.

Many just don't have the time and energy to keep up with all the marketing and social media they know they should be doing. They need a way to get lots of quality prospects, quickly and consistently, without spending hours upon hours marketing themselves. Others have told me they don't have a website, but want to get it right the first time and not waste any money on something that just won't work.

Chapter 10 will help you – How to Find a Good Internet Marketing company.

Conclusion

In this chapter we learned the difference between Brand/Image advertising and Direct Response advertising. We learned that unless you're a huge corporation the way to make money with your Marketing and Advertising is to do Direct Response advertising only. And we learned the crucial ingredients of any Direct Response marketing piece.

The next chapter talks about the incredible power of educating your prospects. It provides step-by-step instructions on how you can use this technique to position yourself as the "Go To Expert" for buying and selling real estate in your area.

CHAPTER 6
THE POWER OF EDUCATING YOUR PROSPECTS

"When I was younger, carrier pigeons like me were on the cutting edge of wireless communication technology. Unfortunately, I never bothered to update my training!"

Times have changed. Many of the old ways of sales and marketing don't work anymore, or don't work as well. Prospects are more sophisticated. They've seen it all before. And the demands they have on them from every corner make them self-centered and impatient, even rude if you're not completely open with them or if they feel their time has been wasted.

We have to learn new techniques that tell prospects what they want to hear. Being a true expert in an area opens up the opportunity for you to teach every one of your prospects to be an expert themselves. That's what they really want.

Most people don't want to spend hundreds of thousands or millions of dollars because someone else said it would be good. They want to quickly and easily learn the right information to make the best decision themselves.

People don't want to be sold. They want to buy.

The moment people sense that you're trying to sell them they turn off, they look down on you and they resist, even if it's only by losing interest in what you're saying. However, when you are educating them, giving them information of real value, they become genuinely interested. And in their eyes you instantly become the expert who is helping them accomplish their goals. They need you.

In this chapter we'll talk about the advantages of educating your prospects and provide step-by-step instructions on how top agents position themselves as experts in the eyes of prospects, both on their websites and in person.

A. The Incredible Hidden Power Of Positioning

Having a great deal of genuinely valuable information on your website about your area of specialization proves in writing that you are the expert in that area. It's undeniable, something people can talk about to their friends and associates with confidence. Your prospects and clients will start asking you general questions about real estate, and even questions about other areas, because they see you as an expert.

The most important benefit of educating your prospects is that every time one of them succeeds they become your advocate. Before long you have an army of evangelists

enthusiastically spreading the best kind of word of mouth
about you and your services.

There are a number of reasons why educating prospects is a powerful marketing technique:

1. They respect you more.

2. They trust you more.

3. It establishes your personal brand.

4. They will send you more referrals.

5. They become more loyal. They won't try to sell
    their home by themselves or deal with someone
    else.

B. Take the Focus Off Yourself

One of the most important aspects of having your
prospects see you as an expert is your attitude. But I'm not
talking about confidence or positioning. I'm talking about
your focus. Ask yourself "When you talk to prospects are
you trying to help them succeed or trying to help yourself
succeed?" It's a subtle but profound shift that can make
your business take off like a rocket.

When you focus on your clients it gives you the humility and sensitivity that true service providers have. People
are drawn to you. You're more approachable because they
don't have to fight their way through your ego to get your
attention. People can sense at an intuitive level that you are
focusing on their needs. They are more open to your suggestions and more likely to follow your recommendations.

C. Step-by-step Instructions on How to Give an Edu-
    cational Presentation to Get Listings

One of the best ways to attract new listings is to give

an educational presentation. And recording it to video makes great content for your website that can bring you new listings for years to come. We recommend developing an educational presentation called something like "10 ways you can get $10,000 more for your home" or a title you feel will get attention, and that you can deliver real value on.

1. **Promotion**

    You can print a simple but nice looking flyer and have it delivered to every residence in your area. In addition to the name of your presentation, your photo, your contact information, complete information about the venue you've chosen, the flyer should say something like "Free Educational Seminar - Two dates only. Limited Seating. Call now to reserve".

    Be sure to stress the word "Educational". And of course, when people call to reserve their seat you get everyone's name and phone number.

    You could also buy an ad in the local community newspaper or community websites to publicize your event depending on your budget. Make sure your presentation is not the same evening as a sporting event, the Academy Awards, or popular event like that.

2. **Venue**

    Then you rent a room at the local community centre or a nice hotel in your area. If people don't show you call them afterward and let them know they can watch a recording of the presentation on your website.

    You can send them the link to the page on your website that has the video if they give you their mailing address. Or even better, you can email them the link to it if they give you their email address. That will be easier for them. Either way you now have a way to reach them in the future.

3. **Content**
   a. **FSBO**

FSBOs accounted for only 9% of home sales in 2013, so it's not a major consideration. But because the purpose of the presentation is to get listings, we recommend that part of your presentation talk about the advantages of using a real estate agent. You could say things like "The 2014 NAR Profile of Home Buyers and Sellers says that in 2013 the typical agent-assisted home sold for 25% more than the typical FSBO home".

These are the problems FSBO sellers complain about the most, in order of importance. You could talk about these problems, without explaining how to solve them:

   i.   Understanding and properly handling paperwork.

   ii.   Getting the right price.

   iii.   Preparing and fixing up the home for sale.

   iv.   Selling their home within the planned length of time.

   v.   Having enough time to devote to all aspects of the sale.

vi. Helping the buyer obtain financing.

vii. Attracting potential buyers.

b. **Statistics**

It's good to start out with statistics about whatever market you are specializing in. It gives your whole presentation credibility. It makes it seem important, like you are a genuine knowledgeable expert.

It's also a good idea to show data on your market over a long period of time. People are generally impressed with this kind of market data because it shows trends. For example, you could show them how much the average value of a home in your area has increased over the last 20 years. And if it makes your area look good you could compare it with other areas of town.

If you can't find the data you want for your specific area it's OK to show data about a larger area as long as you say something about how that data relates to your area. Perhaps you could have data on the cost of building an elevated deck vs the increase in selling price. And you could say something about elevated decks being popular in this area so it's good to have one. Usually people want what everyone else has.

Use as many specific figures as you can. They are much more credible than approximations or price ranges. Specific information about your market is more interesting than about individual houses that people might not be interested in, unless those houses are examples that illustrate your points.

c. **Slides**

Prepare some PowerPoint slides. It's good to use lots of photos, images and graphs that illustrate your points.

Sometimes an audience member will ask if you will make your PowerPoint slides available. We don't recommend it. You don't want them turning up in somebody else's presentation. If somebody asks just smile and tell them you can't make the slides available, but they can watch the video of the entire presentation on your website as many times as they like.

Ideally you would have real life examples of properties you've sold to illustrate each of your points. Then you could say things like "This is a three bedroom home that we (did this to in order to increase the value of the property.)" However, you can still have a very educational presentation that is of genuine value to the audience even if you weren't involved in any of those sales.

You might start your presentation by pointing out home improvements that do NOT increase the selling price enough to cover the cost.

4. **Getting to Know You**
When people arrive smile and greet them at the door. Be friendly so they see you as someone they can talk to, someone who will listen to them. Being a real estate agent is about making as many friends

as you can. This is another opportunity to practice being interested in other people, and in listening.

Also, it's good to learn about your audience, what they're most interested in learning, and what kind of people they are. Ask things like "What are you hoping to get from tonight's presentation?" This will help you know what to emphasize in your talk.

5. **Audio and Video**

Someone should come with you to videotape your presentation so you can put it on your website.

It's important to wear a lapel microphone, record a few words of your presentation before everyone arrives as a test, and play the video back to make sure it sounds good, with the correct volume not fuzzy. The strange thing about videos is that it's easier to watch a video with poor quality video than with poor quality sound.

In addition, it's important to have some kind of public address system, that is, a microphone connected to a speaker so everyone in the audience will hear you. Please don't try to do it without. You can buy an inexpensive Karaoke machine from The Source that works great as a portable Public Address system. So that means you'll be wearing a lapel microphone to record the sound for the video, and at the same time speaking into a microphone you're holding in your hand for the audience.

It's also good to rent some cold lighting for the evening that points at the front of the room where you'll be standing. You'll look more professional and the video will be better quality.

You can buy a good LCD projector for $300 to $500, and a portable rollup screen for less than $200. Of course you'll need a laptop with Microsoft PowerPoint or similar software installed. If your projector doesn't come with a remote control that will change your PowerPoint slides from anywhere in the room, you can buy one that doubles as a laser pointer for $50.

It's good to bring a three pronged extension cord and a power bar. You might want to put some of your business cards and a bottle of water in with them. Don't forget to arrive an hour early, set everything up and make sure it's all working. If something isn't working that will give you time to either find the solution or replace the defective part.

6. **Presenting**

45 to 60 minutes is a good length for your presentation. Unless you are a professional speaker with scintillating content you'll have trouble keep your audience interested for longer. And if it's much shorter than that they won't feel it's been worth their time to come out.

It's good to dress like an expert, best to wear a suit and tie. You should start your presentation with an introduction to yourself and your credentials just to reinforce the fact that you are an authority. Give the title of your talk and what the audience will learn from it.

But remember, as soon as you mention even one phrase that sounds like you're a salesman, if you start to say how good you are, how hard you work for your clients, or talk about your 12 point marketing plan, people will instantly turn off. It's an Educational Presentation. Some of the naïve people in the audience will even feel tricked. "I thought I was coming to an educational seminar, not a 60 minute sales pitch."

This presentation will only be effective if you don't sell. If you consistently talk like an expert who doesn't need their business, serious prospects will come to you asking you to help them accomplish their goals. Of course you're doing it for business, to establish yourself as an authority in the field, but you're not begging for their listing. You're very busy already.

7. **Speaking**
Speak clearly, and try not to turn your back on your audience. It's good to vary your talking speed and your tone, serious sometimes, humorous others. It's also good to pause once in a while for a moment to get people's attention, and to emphasize whatever you just said.

Don't read a script unless you absolutely have to. If you want to read parts of your presentation word for word you can put the words on your PowerPoint slides and read them as the audience is seeing them. It's more effective if you can put just a few words about your main points on your slides to remind you what you want to talk about, and speak off the cuff about each point. But don't go off on a tangent. Stick to the point.

Rehearse, rehearse, rehearse until you look like

you're calm and relaxed. I can't stress this enough. Professional speakers rehearse until long after they're completely bored with their presentation. It's good to video your rehearsals. Then watch them and look for things you can improve. But don't worry about trying to be perfect. Just do the best you can. It will be good enough.

8. **Audience Participation**
    If you can get people participating in any way they will enjoy your presentation more, they will learn more from it, and less of them will fall asleep. While you're giving your presentation ask everyone to raise their hands in response to your questions. And raise your hand very high when you ask a question to show them what to do.

    "How many people here tonight live in (your area)?" Raise your hand so they raise their hands.

    "How many people have had that happen to them?" Raise your hand so they raise their hands.

    "Anybody here know what I'm talking about?" Raise your hand high so they raise their hands.

    To reinforce your important points you can raise your hand and ask -

    "Make sense?"

    Another thing you can do is say something like "OK, now we're going to find a partner and take 2 minutes, How long? (wait for their answer), to talk about what we think are the best selling points of our house. After 2 minutes we'll switch partners". Then later you can do the same thing and have them talk about the problems they might have selling their home. Be sure to tell them when 2 minutes is up, so they switch partners. And you need to make sure everyone has a partner.

If someone asks a question you don't want to talk about at the time, just say "Can I talk to you after the presentation about that?" If they say they can't stay after the presentation ask them to write their name and phone number on a piece of paper and you'll call them tomorrow. Don't forget to call.

9. **Door Prizes**

You could phone a few moving companies, home staging companies, and handyman companies. Tell them you're giving a presentation to people who are interested in selling their homes, and suggest that if they would donate a door prize you'd be happy to promote their business during the presentation, and leave some of their brochures on a table by the door.

It's now in their best interests to have as many people at your event as possible, so ask them if there is anything they can do to promote the event, maybe send an email to their customers, include a note in the invoices they mail out, leave some of your flyers on their counter, put it on their website, anything.

If they are OK with sending an email to their customers tell them that to make it easy you can write the email, if they wish, and send it to them so they can send it out. That way you can make sure it says what you want it to say. Tell them you'll send them a video of what you say about them during your event.

Having door prizes is one way to get your audience to stay right to the end. Of course you have to give them one half of a numbered ticket when they come in, and at the beginning of your talk let everybody know the draw will be at the end of the presentation, and what the prizes are.

It's good if your friend can sit at a table by the door, smile and say hello when people come in, and give them their half of the door prize ticket. This is a very good time to write down their name and phone number. You can have some of your business cards on the table also.

10. Topics for Other Presentations

It's also a good idea to do presentations on topics like these, and put them on your website as a series of pages with headlines and interesting visuals.

- Everything you need to know to be an expert at selling homes in (your area)

- Everything you need to know to be an expert home buyer in (your area)

11. Better Next Time

After every presentation, no matter how successful, sit down and ask yourself how it could be improved next time. Write your points down and save them in a place of their own so you can refer to them later. This is the most effective way to ensure you only get better and better.

D. Educating Your Prospects Without Public Speaking

If you don't want to give a public talk you can record

a video of your presentation in your home. That way you can edit and redo sections of it as many times as you like. Whatever you do, putting the videos on your website is an absolute must.

There are a number of considerations when putting video on your website. Here are a few things you can do to get the most mileage from them:

1. Upload them to your YouTube.com account.

2. Make them "Public".

3. Put your keyword phrase in the title.

4. Put Annotations on the video that include your keyword phrase.

5. Do not "Monetize" your video or YouTube will put ads for other companies over your video while it's playing or at the end. It doesn't look good.

6. In the Description of your video include your main keyword phrase once, include a link to your website in this format http://www. topagentinternetmarketing.com. You must include the http://. Include the Name, Address, Phone number of your website (NAP) the same way as it's listed on your Google+ account.

7. Don't buy "Views", but it's good to have a few so that when strangers find it by searching on You-Tube they'll think it's popular. Send an email to your friends and relatives asking them to watch at least the first 8 seconds of it. That's what You-Tube counts as a "View".

8. You could send out another direct mail piece to your area announcing the new video on your

website. Don't forget to make it very easy to find from your homepage.

9. Have someone transcribe the text from your video so you can give it to your website designer with your PowerPoint slides and ask her to make it into a series of colorful pages for your website. These new pages will attract a lot of traffic from people looking for this information on Google.

10. We recommend you promote each of your videos one at a time with Facebook pay per click ads, to see how much traffic they each draw to your website.

E. Walk the Walk

I'm sure you realized long ago that this is not a get rich quick system. What we're talking about here is a system that if applied properly will bring you a life of abundance and be good for everyone concerned. To teach others to be an expert you'll have to become an expert yourself. You'll need to learn as much as you can about your area.

Start going to restaurants, parks, and businesses in your area. If you have time it's good to talk to business owners. Ask them what their specialty is, what they're best at. It may not be apparent from looking at their business. Ask them why they opened their store here, what they like about the area.

You could go to your City Hall and talk to the Planning Department to find out what's happening in your area over the next few years, for example, sewer line upgrades, major buildings going up, roads for new land developments.

You want to learn whatever you need to learn in order to ensure that people who buy from you or ask you to sell their home are getting the best value for their money in the long term. For example:

a. You can explain the most interesting things to do and see in your area.

b. You can ask about their interests, and the interests of their children, and provide information about clubs and local companies who service those interests.

c. You can offer them the names of great companies you've used before, or who have a good reputation, and provide services they may need in the future, such as:

- Home decorating
- Lawn and Garden care
- Home renovating
- Swimming pool installation
- Painting
- Plumbing
- Electrician
- Furniture sales

- Carpet sales
- Drapery sales
- Dry Cleaning
- Babysitting
- Doctor
- Dentist
- House cleaning
- Hardware Store
- Post office
- Good restaurants

Keep in mind that if they have a good experience with one of your recommendations they'll trust your other recommendations, and the opposite is also true. If you're not sure the company is good don't recommend them. It's good to do business with them at least once to see for yourself.

Another thing to remember is that every one of the companies above that you refer business to can be a great source of referrals for you if you cultivate your relationship well, and always let them know when you've referred somebody to them.

F. How To Use The Local Board of Trade

As part of your personal brand as an expert in your area it would be very good to join a committee on the local Chamber of Commerce or Board of Trade. But you have to do it right or you'll be wasting your time.

Just going to lunches probably will bring you little or no benefit. With clubs and associations the saying "You get out of it what you put into it" should be your guiding philosophy. The best way to receive benefit from your membership is to find out who is on their committees and what their day job is.

You can talk to the head of a number of committees about what the committee does and how much time is required. Then join the committee that has people on it you want to become friends with. This is the key.

The way to become real friends with people is to work with them for a number of months or years toward a common goal. Over time, if you do what you say you're going to do, and do the right thing even when nobody is looking, good people on the committee will become real friends. A year or two of committee work like this can be very good for your career in real estate sales.

Conclusion

This chapter discussed the benefits of becoming a genuine expert on your area of specialization, and of educating prospects in a way that proves you are the agent they need to deal with. Usually, if you empower people to do it themselves, they will ask you to do it for them.

In the next chapter I talk about my personal story, how I got into internet marketing in the first place and what it takes to be successful doing internet marketing for real estate agents.

CHAPTER 7
KEN LAPP – WHY DID HE DO IT?

© Randy Glasbergen / glasbergen.com

GLASBERGEN

"Which is better for soul searching, Google, Yahoo or Bing?"

've had to do a lot of soul searching in my time, and the internet is an important part of my life. I thought it might be good to tell part of my personal story so you understand how I came to be good at internet marketing for real estate agents.

Although most people would think of my early years as a sad story, I think of them as an adventure story because they have a happy ending. And of course many people lived through much worse. I mention them here only because they led me directly to success.

A. Life As a Two Dimensional Figure
My father terrorized the whole family, and completely

dominated everybody. One time he bought my mother a new set of kitchen chairs. Later that evening when they had a disagreement he smashed every one of them to splinters on the kitchen floor. Another time when the family was eating dinner at the kitchen table he pointed a finger at me and growled "Don't you even THINK anything bad about me!"

My mother had been a nurse, so I was clean and well fed. But I felt like a ghost in our house, invisible. I received no affection, no praise, and no respect from either of my parents. And the only time I received attention, other than when I was being terrorized, was when my father was telling me how I could have done something better.

He was what my school history books called "An Absolute Ruler". He made every decision for everybody in the family. I had no feeling of self-worth, and of course, no confidence.

The strange thing about my dad was that he didn't set out to be a terrible father. He was actually doing the best he could at the time. He enrolled my sister and I in swimming lessons, gave us piano lessons, and we had family sing-a-longs around the piano while he played. I don't think he was ever with a woman other than my mother. He didn't drink or do drugs, and he worked hard every day to provide for the family. I learned later that he'd also had an unhappy childhood.

When he was about 70 he told me that until he was 42 years old he thought other people were two-dimensional figures. He was the Retail Sales Manager at BCTV in Vancouver, and one of his salesmen had a heart attack. That was the first time in his life he started to realize that other people had feelings and lives of their own.

Gradually over the years he learned more and more about being a good human being, until just before he died he really was a wonderful person, completely concerned about other people. It's very strange that the same person who was such an example of what I never want to be, was also an example of what I hope to be.

B. Hiding Behind My Computer

Because he was very successful in advertising sales and had a number of contacts in the business, at the beginning of my career he helped me get a job in that field. I was outrageously successful, and made big money in my early twenties.

The strange part of the situation was that it was always an act. I never "owned" my success. I was only acting how I thought a $100,000 a year salesman would act. Inside I was still full of fear and feelings of inadequacy. After a few years of making big money I started to self-destruct. I was rebelling against the oppression in my childhood, and I indulged in many types of excess.

Gradually I got out of sales because with no confidence it was hard to deal with people. A salesman not only needs to believe in what he's selling, he needs to believe in himself. I got into Marketing Consulting so I could spend more time on research and writing reports, and at one point started up and managed a nationally accredited in-house advertising agency for an old client. That wasn't so bad because people had to come to me.

But even that became hard after a while so I decided to learn how to use a computer and build myself a website. At that point I wasn't even thinking about it as internet marketing. I just wanted some way to do business without having to meet people. I wanted to hide.

I had an eye for color and design, so I was good at making websites. I was happy to be working at home alone, and I worked long and hard for many years. Often I'd look up and be surprised to see it was 11 pm. It didn't take me long to figure out that the way for customers to find my website was to get it onto page one of Google.

In those days it was much easier than it is now. I became good at getting clients to come to me through my website, and my business grew steadily. After a few years I had four desks and computers in my dining room, and another person on my laptop at the dining room table.

C. Recovery and Traditional Chinese Qigong

I had lived so many years depressed and unhappy. One

day I decided I was going to live at least long enough to enjoy as many happy years as I'd had unhappy years. I knew there was a way I could heal and live a happy life - I just had to find it. By reading a huge number of self-help books, writing my thoughts in a personal journal, and taking every kind of counselling and personal growth course imaginable I did actually make slow but steady progress over the next 20 years.

And every time I made a little progress I told myself that all I had to do was keep going and it was inevitable that I would be completely healed one day. Then I would be happy.

One day I saw a TV documentary on the PBS program "NOVA" about bio-feedback. Essentially it was scientists showing how to train your mind to heal your body. I searched on the internet for "bio feedback" and found a Vancouver website for a group that practiced Yan Xin Qigong®, pronounced "Yan Shin CheeGong".

I went to one of their meetings, and in 1998 started learning it. It's a Chinese meditative practice based on Traditional Chinese Medicine. It's about healing and learning to live a better life by absorbing "Qi", which is the Chinese name for vital life energy. I can say unequivocally that it changed my life.

It has nothing to do with religion. It's only a practice. The teacher, Dr. Yan Xin, is a genuinely humble man with no interest in fame or wealth. He teaches independence, personal responsibility, service to others and doing your best never to harm or even offend anybody. He's conducted many scientific experiments that have been published in peer reviewed English language scientific journals, in order to prove the objective existence of Qi and the power of Traditional Chinese Qigong.

From Yan Xin Qigong® I learned that negativity was my biggest problem, that the road to happiness is paved with positive thoughts, words, and deeds. You still know the negative things are there. You just don't pay them as much attention. I learned not to blame others for my problems, but fix them myself.

Yan Xin Qigong® wasn't always easy, but I never gave up, and after a number of years my healing and rate of personal growth increased significantly. Gradually my confidence came back, I started to enjoy life again, and I was good at sales once more. I even started giving talks around town about SEO and how to make money with your website.

D. A Chance But Fateful Meeting

When people ask me how I started specializing in internet marketing for real estate agents I tell them it happened by chance, if you believe in chance. My upstairs neighbour in those early years was a fellow by the name of Ray Giesbrecht, the BC Sales Manager for MyRealPage. com, a company from Winnipeg that provides inexpensive but robust templated websites to real estate agents and brokers.

He and I got along well so when one of his clients asked him about getting high rankings on Google he referred them to me. Since that time we've both moved out of that building but Ray is still with MyRealPage and I'm still doing Internet Marketing for real estate agents. We've both become very successful. Over the years real estate agents and brokers came to us from all over Canada and the United States looking for success in internet marketing. If you're going to use a company that provides templated websites you must ensure you have easy access to the background code on your website pages. I could tell you some real life horror stories about some of our clients who didn't. We had a client one time, one of the top agents in Canada, who'd been using one of those companies who don't provide access for many years.

He had so much information on his website about his geographic area, his team, and his services, he'd invested so much time and money for so many years getting that company to build custom functions on his website, that regardless of how unhappy he was with their service he just couldn't leave them. It would cost him too much to build the website again.

One time he asked them to make a change to his website. They quoted him $1,150 and said it would take three days. We could have made the same change to a custom WordPress website in 45 minutes.

E. Dan Lok

I've been privileged to partner in my business with Dan Lok. He has large, successful companies coming to him from around the world asking for help with their marketing. And he's taken many companies like Top Agent Internet Marketing to the next level.

His story is not all tea and roses either. He came to Canada from Hong Kong at the age of 14 without a word of English. He was bullied and alone for many years. He failed at his first 13 businesses, but since then has had at least 15 straight successes. He's written a dozen business books, some of which are Amazon best-sellers.

His book F.U. Money is genuinely inspiring. I highly recommend it. He teaches that conventional wisdom is almost always wrong. He has many sayings, called "Lok-isms". My favourite is "Life is unfair, business is unfair, people are unfair. Get over it!" He's smart, humble, has piercing insight, and is genuinely interested in helping people.

It's part of my business to stay on the leading edge of internet marketing and marketing in general. So I go to a lot of conferences and seminars. Some are a waste of time but usually there's something I can learn, and it's just something I have to do.

So I've seen many high powered marketing people speak. I can tell you that I've never seen any of them who are more interested in what's really working in the business world right now than Dan Lok. That's his only interest.

F. The Source Of My Motivation

The point in telling my story here is to explain where I got the motivation to work as hard as I did for as long as I did to become an SEO expert, and how it happened that I became an expert at helping real estate agents. I'm hoping that from my story you will gain some understanding about who I am and how we do business.

- Feeling invisible as a child made me want to connect with people in a meaningful way and provide them with real value.

- Being constantly criticized when I was young made me want to be very good at what I do.

- Being depressed for so many years forced me to become a person who never gives up, and gave me passion for personal growth, for being the best I can be.

- My years in Yan Xin Qigong® taught me that happiness comes from being positive, from improving yourself, and from being of service to others.

- My chance meeting with Ray Giesbrecht at MyRealPage started me on the road to helping a great many real estate agents make money on the internet.

G. How To Be Successful At Internet Marketing For Real Estate Agents

Follow these nine steps:

1. Work six or seven days a week for 16 years.

2. Never give up.

3. Understand where Google's ranking criteria started, and stay up-to-date on every major change in their ranking criteria over the years so you understand where they are going, and why.

4. Don't believe everything Google says. Learn by doing, that Google's ranking criteria for small companies and websites is sometimes very different than their criteria for large websites.

5. Read lots of business books and spend hundreds of hours and thousands of dollars every year attending Marketing Conferences and Internet Marketing courses around North America.

6. Don't believe everything you hear at marketing

conferences and courses. Pick and choose what
works for your situation.

7. Do business with all kinds of real estate agents
    and brokers in many different locations.

8. Learn what areas of business you're good at and
    what you're not. Work with other people who
    are good at what you're not so you can spend your
    time doing what you do best.

9. Understand that it's OK to ask for help some-
    times. Find a business coach or mentor who is
    successful doing what he teaches. The most suc-
    cessful people I know have many mentors.

Conclusion

In this chapter we learned about my background and
how I got to where I am today, as well as what it takes to
be successful in this business. In the next chapter we'll talk
about the more technical aspects of Search Engine Optimization.

CHAPTER 8
FOR COMPUTER GEEKS ONLY

"I memorized all of my e-mail addresses, passwords, and PIN numbers...but now I don't remember my name!"

Search Engine Optimization is a business of details. There are so many of them and some are absolutely crucial. Sometimes if you get one detail wrong all of your other SEO work is wasted. It's helps to be patient and thorough, and have a reliable system you can trust.

To describe each of the technical issues mentioned here in detail would require many books. And this is only a small portion of the issues you could get into. This chapter is a beginner's guide to the technical issues that need to be addressed in order to get high rankings on Google for your website.

I've tried to explain each point in simple language anybody can understand. But this chapter is not for everybody. You don't even need to read it unless you're planning to do it all yourself, or you want to learn as much about SEO as you can. Any good SEO company will have a solid grasp of these issues, and make sure they're in order for every one of their clients.

A. The Incredible Power of Google Analytics

The word "Analytics" means analyzing website statistics. This will be your most important tool for improving the effectiveness of your website. It can tell you many things, over any period of time you wish. For example:

1. How many people visited each page of your website, and how long they stayed.

2. What geographic area they came from.

3. What websites and search engines they came from.

4. What search terms, that is, keywords they input into the different search engines.

5. What page most people leave your website from.

6. What people are searching for on your website, if you have a "Search" function.

7. How many people visited your website with their smart phone.

You can use this information to know what content on your website is more interesting to your website visitors, and how to guide visitors through your website to where you want them to go.

Anybody with a website can sign up for a free Analytics account on Google. You'll have to verify the website you're applying for is actually yours. The two easiest ways Google asks you to do that is to add a Meta Tag to the

HTML code of your homepage in the Head section, and to upload an HTML file to your website server. If you sign up for a free Google AdWords account as well you can integrate it with your Google Analytics account and gain even more useful information about how people use your website. You can do that whether you spend any money on AdWords or not. You just need to set up an account.

If you do decide to invest some money in Google AdWords you can analyze the effectiveness of your ads and your Landing Pages in great depth, showing which ones are making money and which ones are not. We'll discuss a lot more about Google AdWords and Landing Pages in Chapter 9.

B. Mastering Google's Webmaster Tools

Google Webmaster Tools is another free and very important tool you'll need to use on an ongoing basis to improve your traffic and the effectiveness of your website. If your website works well Google will give it better rankings. When you set up your account, once again you'll have to verify the website you're applying for is actually yours.

These are some important things you should be doing with your Google Webmaster Tools account:

1. XML sitemap

Your website needs an XML sitemap to make sure Google finds all your pages. If Google can't find all of the content on your website they might not be giving it the rankings it deserves.

To easily create a good XML sitemap go to www. xml-sitemaps.com. Enter your url, save the file it creates to your computer, then upload it to the root directory of your website. The "root" directory just means the main directory. If you have videos on your website you should add them to your Sitemap in a specific way. Please see this page on Google's support website for directions on adding videos to your XML sitemap. https://support.google.com/webmasters/answer/80472?hl=en

Once your sitemap has been uploaded to your website Google will tell you how many of your pages it has indexed. When we say "indexed" we just mean that Google has found the page, saved it in their memory banks, and put it in a place with labels so they'll know where to find it quickly when they want it.

If Google hasn't indexed all your pages it's usually because you have duplicate content on those pages, you haven't given them unique Title and Description Tags, or no other websites have linked to them so Google doesn't seem them as being important.

2. Robots.txt file

If you have pages on your website that you don't want everyone in the world to have access to, you can use the robots.txt file to limit Google's access to them. Google and most other search engines will respect your robots.txt file, but some may not. If you have sensitive information on your website you should make those pages password accessible only.

Google provides a robots.txt file generator right on their website, and also a tester in case you've made changes to it by yourself and want to check your work.

3. **If you change your domain name**

   If you change the domain name of your website you must take a number of steps to let Google know what you've done or your rankings will crash. After your new website is up and running you'll need to:

   a. Create a 301 redirect for every page on your old website to tell Google what page on your new website that content is now located.

   b. Verify your new website.

   c. Select your new domain name in the Change of Address section.

4. **Canonical domain name**

   It's better to decide whether your website will be known as http://www.yourwebsite.com or http://yourwebsite.com. Google stated a number of years ago that they treat subdomains as separate websites, and www is actually a subdomain of your website. To avoid possible duplicate content problems you should choose one or the other and direct all users there.

5. **404 Page Not Found**

   In your Webmaster Tools account you can see how many 404 Not Found errors visitors to your website have seen, and how many broken links there are. There are many possible reasons for 404 errors. But more than a few 404's on your website is not good, because Google wants to give high rankings to websites that work. You should periodically check and repair any you find.

6. **Load time**
   Google will tell you how long your website takes to appear when people come to it for the first time. In recent years Google has given higher rankings to websites with faster load times. For smaller websites it's not a major consideration, but it's still is a consideration.

C. Meta Tags

Properly writing the Meta Tags mentioned here is among the most important "on-page" Search Engine Optimization work you can do. "On-page" simply means SEO work done on your website. "Off-page" SEO is work done anywhere else.

There are many different Meta Tags that perform a wide variety of functions. Some will help your pages display well on Facebook, some will do the same on Twitter. And there are many more. These are some that are important for SEO.

Meta Tags are inserted into the "Head" section of your web pages, as opposed to the "Body" section, that is, in the background HTML code of the pages. The Body of a web page contains the text, images and functions that you see on the page. The Head section is usually seen only by the internet browser you're using, and by search engine crawlers.

When you're working on your Meta Tags please remember what we said in Chapter 2 about Google's ranking algorithm. It is unbelievably smart at knowing whether you've got too many keywords on your pages. That includes your Meta Tags. If you have too many keywords your rankings will be penalized.

1. **Title Tags**

   The Title Tag of a page is perhaps the most important place to include keywords and phrases to let Google know what that page on your website is about. It's also important because it's what Google uses as a link to your website in their search results. The Title Tags for each page on your website will all be somewhat similar because every page on your website will talking about something to do with your specialty. However, each Title Tag should be a little bit different on every page.

   Ideally Title Tags are 50 to 60 characters long, including spaces. But Google doesn't actually count the characters. They count the pixels. They display a maximum of 512 pixels of your Title Tag on search results pages. It's not a major catastrophe if your Title Tag is longer than that. It just means that it won't all be displayed.

2. **Description Tags**

   Even though Google said some time ago that they don't count the Description Tag as one of their ranking criteria they are still tremendously important. The Description Tag is the text that Google displays under the link to your website in their search results. So this is the text that people use to decide whether to come to your website or not.

   And as mentioned before, the Click Through Rate of your website in the organic listings is one of

Google's ranking criteria. Your Description Tag should contain the most interesting, most exciting, most compelling reasons why anybody would want to visit your website.

The more compelling your Description Tag the higher your Click Through Rate will be, and the more people will come to your website. As with your Title Tag, your Description Tags should be a little different on every page of your website, because every page is talking about a slightly different topic.

3. **Keyword Tags**

   Google said many years ago they don't use the Keyword Meta Tag as a ranking factor so it's best if you don't use it at all. Google's ranking algorithm is very sensitive to the number of keywords on a page. Having a Keyword Meta Tag and putting keywords in it is tempting the fates. Why do it if you don't have to?

4. **Alt Tags**

   The information in the Alt Tag of an image or photograph is what most internet browsers, such as Chrome, Mozilla Firefox, and Internet Explorer display if the image cannot be displayed on the web page for some reason.

   It's supposed to give the viewer of the page an idea of what the photo is about. It is a good idea to include keywords or words related to your keywords in the Alt text of your images. But again, don't put too many keywords in too many places or

Google will lower your rankings.

D. Our Favorite WordPress Plugins

WordPress has a number of useful plugins. After many years of working with them, these are the best we've found:

1. **Yoast**

   The actual name of this plugin is "WordPress SEO" by Yoast, but it's commonly called just "Yoast". This plugin will perform a wide variety of SEO related functions on your website. We highly recommend it.

   Its only drawback is that it hasn't kept up with Google's Panda and Hummingbird algorithm changes. Its recommendations will encourage you to include too many keywords in your pages.

2. **Contact 7**

   This is a very robust and easy-to-use way to create forms on your website, so that visitors to your website can request more information in general, or give you their contact information in return for a special market report, or request to be contacted.

3. **Akismet**

   This is a good plugin for reducing the spam you receive from your website blog. The commercial version costs $10 per month. We find it's well worth it.

4. **CoSchedule**

   This plugin is very good for automatically posting your blogs to your social media accounts. It also costs $10 per month.

E. Dealing With Spam

Technically, spam is any kind of unwanted communication on the internet. Google views keyword stuffing on your website as spam. In email, any unsolicited commercial email is considered spam. When we talk about website spam we're talking about forms that are filled out with junk and submitted.

You must have at least one form on your website. It's better to have many. When someone fills out one of your forms the information they typed into the form is emailed to you. The problem is that there are a number of computer programmers who write programs with the sole purpose of scanning the internet looking for forms on websites, and filling them out with junk just to irritate website owners.

One way to stop all or most of the spam from your website forms is to have your website developer install a "captcha" on each form. A captcha makes it so people filling out the form have to enter the correct characters in the right text box before they can submit the form. Unfortunately it's a proven fact that less real prospects will fill out your form if you add a captcha, so we recommend against it.

Marketing is firstly about making it as easy as possible for prospects to contact you, and only secondly about the convenience of the website owner. In order to guarantee you don't miss any bona fide prospects wanting to do business with you we recommend allowing all the spam forms submitted on your website through your spam filter. Then just delete them in your email program.

This means that in the first few months that your website is live to the internet it's good to check your email spam filter every day or as often as you can to see if any real forms got caught there. Each email system will have its own method you can use to train it that forms from your website should not be sent to your spam filter. If you use Gmail you'll have to tell it a number of times. In our experience you'll get a lot of spam for a few days or perhaps a few weeks and then it drops off to nothing. Perhaps the spammers just get bored and move on.

F. Good Resources

1. **WordPress.org**
   This website is a great WordPress resource. There are 37,915 WordPress plugins available on that website, among many other WordPress resources.

2. **Morris Real Estate Marketing Group**
   Morris are the leaders in turnkey, done for you Marketing Systems for Referral Marketing and Community Marketing. Morris Real Estate Marketing Group has been in business for over twenty years, and has thousands of real estate agents as long term clients throughout North America. Find out more about them at their website - http://www.morrismarketinggroup.com

3. **MyRealPage.com**
   MyRealPage provides fully functional websites for real estate agents and brokers very inexpensively, that include MLS IDX. They've been in business a long time and are good at what they do. They also provide a very good IDX WordPress plugin for custom WordPress websites. Find out more at - http://myrealpage.com

G. 13 Tools We Use Regularly

This is not meant to be a thorough analysis of all the pros and cons of the software mentioned here. These are just some of the software tools I find useful that you might not be aware of, or that I use in an unusual way. Take them as insider tips on things we've learned from 16 years of trying many different options.

1. **Camtasia by TechSmith**

   Camtasia is a fully robust program to record your computer screen and your voice through a microphone at the same time. It's the standard in its field. Perfect for tutorials, Help videos, or long and complicated demonstrations or explanations. $299 USD.

2. **Jing by TechSmith**

   This is a free tool you can use to record a 5 minute video of your computer monitor screen with your voice-over. Easy to use. Very handy for communicating with contractors or clients when an email or a phone call won't do.

3. **Hubspot Sidekick**

   For $10 a month I receive an instant notification the moment people open my emails, and if I miss something I can check the Sidekick website anytime to find when every email I sent was opened. If I receive a notification that someone has just opened one of my old emails I know they are thinking about me.

4. **Moz.com**

   This is perhaps the most respected source of SEO

information on the web. We pay every month to be Moz Pro members. The Moz toolbar is a very useful addition to Google Chrome. It tells you many things at a glance about each website in the organic search results on Google, including Domain Authority. It's a good way to size up your competition to see how easy or difficult it will be to climb over them in the organic rankings.

5. **Majestic.com**
   We are a paid subscriber. Majestic says they are the largest source of information on backlinks to any website on the internet. Moz also will show you the backlinks to any website, however, the word on the street is that Moz shows you the backlinks that count for your rankings. Majestic shows you them all.

6. **SearchEngineNews.com**
   We are paid members. This website has a great deal of information on how to get high rankings on Google, and quite good paid courses.

7. **BrightLocal.com**
   Not cheap, but very good rank reporting software that includes rankings on the Seven Pack of Google My Business listings with the red dot on the map. Not all rank reporting software does that.

8. **Sound Forge Audio Editor**
   I use this for burning CD's from webinars I've attended so I can listen to them in my car while I'm driving. It resamples from 16,000 Hz to 44,100 Hz quickly and easily. This is important because

most mp3's on the web are 16,000 Hz. But in order
to play them on a CD player they must be 44,100
Hz. About $60 USD.

9. **NetFirms.com**

I like to reserve my domain names at this website
because it offers suggestions on similar names,
because it will reserve .ca domain names, and
because I've never searched for a name here, found
it's available, and then gone back in an hour only
to find it's been taken. Netfirms is good that way.
Not all domain reservation companies are.

10. **Evernote**

We use this software for showing each member of
our team what their current priorities are. Anybody on the team can make changes to the same
lists so staff and contractors check tasks off when
they've been done. It helps us keep track of all the
important details that must be done for each client.

11. **Notepad**

We find this little program very useful. I mentioned it in Chapter 2. Notepad strips the markup
code from text, just leaving the plain text. If you
want to move text from one program to another,
just copy the text from your first program and paste
it into Notepad. Then copy it from Notepad and
paste it into your second program. It also has a
very useful "Find and Replace" function.

You'll find Notepad in the "Accessories" folder of
your Windows computer programs. First click the
round "Start" button in the bottom left corner of

your computer monitor desktop. Then click "All Programs", and "Accessories".

12. **Windows Keyboard Shortcuts**
When you're working on a computer these short-cuts can make your work much easier. When I say "Ctrl+a" I mean holding down the "Ctrl" key and the key for the letter "a" at the same time.

a. "Ctrl+a" will select or highlight everything on the page or document you're working on.

b. "Ctrl+c" will copy any selected or high-lighted text, photo, or graphic.

c. "Ctrl+v" will paste whatever you've copied to wherever your cursor is at the time.

d. "Ctrl+z" will undo your last action in most programs.

e. "Ctrl+y" will redo your last action is some programs.

f. "Ctrl+s" will save your work in most pro-grams.

g. If you drag and drop a file or folder to your desktop while holding down the "Alt" key, it will create a shortcut to the file or folder from your desktop.

h. If you drag and drop a file or folder to your desktop or other folder while holding down the "Ctrl" key, it will copy the file or folder to your desktop.

13. Web Page Load Time Test

We like www.webpagetest.org. It shows you a grade on a number of different aspects of your page and specifically what you need to do to improve.

14. Google Chrome

In case you're not already aware that Google Chrome is the best internet browsing software I wanted to bring it to your attention. Many website developers prefer the tools available on Mozilla Firefox, but Chrome is faster.

If you use any particular software in an uncommon way, or have found a particularly useful tool not on this list, please tell us about it on this page of our website. Maybe we'll include it in the next printing of our book. http://www.topagentinternetmarketing.com/SOLD/tools

Conclusion

This chapter was for people who want to do SEO themselves, or for technical minded people who want to understand more about the work required to get high rankings on Google and use the internet effectively.

The next chapter looks at the pros and cons of Pay Per Click advertising, why it's better than Organic rankings in some cases, why it's not as good in some cases, and how to do it well.

JOIN OUR FREE WEBINAR AS A COMPANION TO THIS BOOK –

★ Register Now due to limited number of participants – Go to http://www.topagentinternetmarketing.com/ FreeWebinar

"How Top Real Estate Agents are Using the Internet to Capture More Leads and Close More Sales"

- See more Real Life Examples

- Learn Advanced Strategies

- Watch the actual concepts and processes described in this book done for you live

- Qualify for a Free One-on-One Consultation ($500 value)

- Enter your name for a Free Website Analysis ($1,200 value)

CHAPTER 9
PAY PER CLICK ADVERTISING

Copyright 2005 by Randy Glasbergen.
www.glasbergen.com

GLASBERGEN

"As an alternative to the traditional 30-year mortgage, we also offer an interest-only mortgage, balloon mortgage, reverse mortgage, upside down mortgage, inside out mortgage, loop-de-loop mortgage, and the spinning double axel mortgage with a triple lutz."

oogle has made their pay per click advertising more and more complicated. To have full functionality in your AdWords account you need to combine it with your Analytics account, and in some cases with your Webmaster Tools account.

To professionals like us who are Certified in both Google AdWords and Analytics it opens up a number of opportunities to provide service to our clients. But for smaller clients trying to manage their own pay per click advertising it must seem very complicated indeed.

In this chapter we'll talk about the basics - how pay per click advertising works, some of the terminology, the advantages and disadvantages, how to get started, how to write an effective ad, managing your ads, and how to make any word people search for show up in your ad. We'll talk about remarketing or retargeting, the advantages of having a special Landing Page and how to build a good one. We'll talk about Google AdSense, that is, making money by having Google ads on your website. We'll talk about some of the major websites that have their own type of ads, and we'll talk about their differences.

A. Does Your Pay Per Click Spend Influence Your Organic Rankings?

A crucial point when talking about Google's pay per click advertising is to understand that they make 98% of their 50 billion dollar annual revenue from it, so it's very important to them. We also need to understand that when more people use Google, Google makes more money, because more people click their ads. That's why their main goal is always to get more people to use their search engine.

Another important point is that Google knows that one of the most important reasons people use their search engine is that they trust their organic rankings. People have faith that if a website is at the top of Google's organic search results it's because it's a good website run by a good company.

Google values that trust tremendously and would never do anything to jeopardize it. If people lost faith in Google's organic rankings less people would use Google and their revenue would go down.

As tempting as it might be for Google to take a bribe and raise one of their large corporate client's organic rankings artificially they would never do it. They're smart enough to know the word would get out eventually and that would be the end of Google. For Google, credibility is everything.

So your website's organic rankings, that is, in the non-paid or natural listings, are not influenced in any way by how much you spend on their pay per click advertising.

This is what we're talking about when we say "organic" listings.

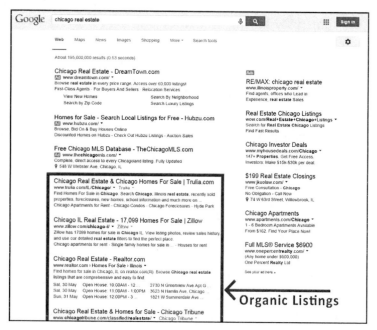

Organic Listings

B. How Pay Per Click Advertising Works

You only pay when somebody clicks your ad and is taken to your website. Something that most people aren't aware of is that you can include your phone number or address in your ad, so people can call you or come to your store without clicking your ad. And yet you only pay when somebody clicks it.

The price you pay for each click is based on a bidding system. You bid against all the other websites that want to have their ad on the search results page for the keyword phrases you're targeting. When somebody clicks your ad Google takes the amount of your bid for that keyword phrase from your credit card.

You pay a different price for every keyword phrase because each phrase has a different number of websites bidding for it. The website that bids the most for each keyword phrase gets to be at the top of the search results page. The website that bids the second highest is second, and so on down.

Google puts the three highest bidding ads at the very top of the search results pages, and only differentiates them from the organic or non-paid listings underneath by including a little yellow square at the top left of each, with the word "Ad" in white letters inside it.

They also put ads down the right side of the page. They are smaller and rectangular, but they are all the same type of pay per click ads. And sometimes they also put another three "Ad" listings at the bottom of the page under the organic listings.

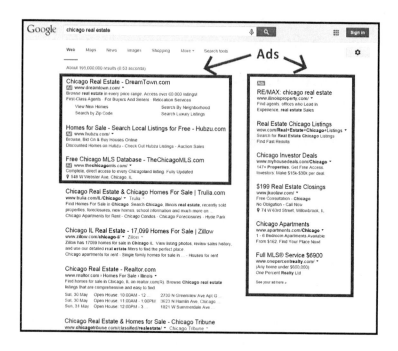

C. Definitions and Acronyms

Pay per click advertising(PPC) is sometimes called "Paid Search", "Sponsored Search", or " Search Engine Marketing"(SEM). Paid Search is the opposite of "Organic Search" or "Search Engine Optimization" (SEO). SEO is concerned with getting people to come to your website from your organic or "not paid" listings on search engines. SEM is concerned with getting people to come to your website from your "paid" ads, that is, your pay per click ads.

D. Advantages of Pay Per Click Advertising

Pay per click advertising has a number of advantages in certain situations over Organic Search Engine Optimization:

1. **Top of the page** - Major search engines put their

pay per click ads right at the top of the search results pages, above the organic listings.

2. **Very quick** - You can get to the top of page one of Google within 24 hours as long as you're willing to pay a higher price for your keywords than all the other ads. PPC can be used to generate traffic to your website while you're waiting for your SEO work to get you top of the organic rankings.

3. **Double exposure** - PPC ads enable you to be on page one of Google more than once. That is, you can have your organic listing on page one of Google for a keyword phrase, and at the same time have one of your pay per click ads on page one of Google for the same keyword phrase. It's more impressive for people who are looking for your service to see you on page one twice.

4. **Testing** – Pay per click advertising can be very good for inexpensively testing many possible keywords to see which will get the most attention, and the most clicks.

5. **Many types of ads** - With Google, in addition to text ads, you can also have display ads with photos, animations, even videos. There are also many sizes and shapes of ads, small rectangular ads, long thin horizontal ads that go across the top or bottom of the page, tall thin skyscraper ads that run down the side of the page, and almost any size you can imagine.

6. **Remarketing** – If you use Display ads you can use Remarketing or Retargeting, to show your ads on many websites to people who've been to your

website. We'll talk more about remarketing later in this chapter.

7. **Contextual** - With Google pay per click you can place your ads not just on Google, but also on websites that have an agreement with Google, that talk about any topic you wish. For example, you can have your ads on websites that talk about real estate as an investment, so you reach prospects at the second level of their buying process.

E. Disadvantages of Pay Per Click Advertising

Pay per click advertising has a number of disadvantages when compared to spending your money on getting high organic rankings. We're certified by Google in their pay per click advertising so we know a lot about it. We've found that with the exception of a few specific situations, overall for our clients the disadvantages of pay per click advertising highly outweigh the advantages.

1. **Less return per dollar** - We've found over 16 years that dollar for dollar, pay per click advertising returns less revenue than spending your money on organic rankings. Our clients receive a greater return per dollar by far from investing in higher organic rankings, than they do from investing in pay per click advertising.

2. **Limited reach** - Only 15% of Google users ever click an ad. People are surprised to hear that, but it's true. 85% of Google users never click an ad, any ad. This means if all you do is pay per click you're bringing a very limited percentage of the market to your website.

3. **Here today, gone tomorrow** - There is no residual ranking equity with pay per click ads like there is with organic rankings. If you've only invested in paid search, the day you stop your ads your website is completely gone from Google. Nobody will find it.

   However, if you've invested in organic rankings and have achieved rankings near the top of page one, even if you stop working on your rankings for a short while your rankings will only deteriorate slowly, not disappear instantly.

4. **Lower quality prospects** - You get a lower quality of prospect from pay per click ads than from high rankings in the organic listings. People know those pay per click ads are ads, and anybody can buy their way to the top. So their expectations that the website will actually have what they're looking for are lower than if it was high in the organic listings. And of course people see what they expect to see.

   Another point is that people trust Google's organic listings. If your website is in the number one spot on page one of the organic search results people think you are the best. That's why, if you are the best, it's important to get your website to the number one spot so the general public is not misdirected to somebody who doesn't give as good service as you do.

   Another reason why pay per click generally result in a lower return on investment is that most websites who buy pay per click ads expect the ads to do the heavy lifting and don't create a special Landing Page. They just use their homepage. Or if they have a Landing Page it's not well done. So people who click their ad are confused when they are taken to a Landing Page that doesn't relate well to the message in the ad. They don't know what to do.

F. How to Get Started in Pay Per Click Advertising On Google

Google makes it easy to sign up for an AdWords account. To find the sign up page just search on Google for "Google Adwords sign up". These steps will get you off to a good start.

1. Think about what you want to say in your Google pay per click ads, for example, "Official guide to selling homes in (your area)."

2. Build a special Landing Page on your website for people to come to who click your ads. Your Landing page should talk about the same issues as your ad, and use the same wording so people know they're in the right place and that they'll find what they're looking for.

3. Sign up for a Google AdWords account.

4. Tell Google the maximum you want to spend each day, and type in your credit card information.

5. Choose the keywords that will trigger your ad being displayed on the Google search results pages.

6. Unless you let Google choose the maximum price you'll pay for each keyword phrase you'll have

to manage each one yourself. For beginners we recommend letting Google do it.

7. Write your ads. It's good to write many ads with different wording because it's very difficult to predict which ad will bring the most results.

8. Tell Google the url of your Landing Page. If you don't have a specially designed Landing Page you can use your homepage. We recommend changing the headings and the first text visitors see on your homepage to the wording in your ad.

9. Choose the geographic area where you want your ads to be seen.

10. You can limit the times of the day when your ads are shown on Google, if you wish.

G. How to Write Pay Per Click Ads That Sell

Google will help you with suggestions when you're writing your ads. There is a maximum number of characters you can use on each line.

1. Decide what you will talk about. What do you have to offer?

2. Decide on your target market. Who are your customers? What are their needs?

3. Decide your goal. What do you want people who see your ads to do - come to your website, phone you, come to your office?

4. What are your most impressive selling points?

5. What's special or different about you or your offering?

6. Be specific and get to the point.

7. Include your most important keywords in the headline of your ad.

8. It's good to have numbers in your ad, and unusual characters, such as *, ^, and #. They attract attention because they're unusual.

9. Have a Call To Action.

10. Be creative with your Display URL. Include keywords.

Here are a couple examples of well written Google AdWords text ads:

$12537 more for your home
www.loveoakbayrealestate.com
We know #^*& secrets learned from 9
years selling homes 12% over asking

Free Educational Seminar*
www.passionforubcrealestate.com
How to be an expert UBC home seller
14 Secrets masters know. Call Now**

H. Managing Your AdWords Pay Per Click Advertising

Of course your ad will get more clicks if it is the first ad on the page, but all of your competition also want to be first so you might get into a bidding war that helps nobody but Google. If that happens it's usually better to take the number 2 or 3 spot on the page.

But even those can be expensive, and unless you have a large budget and a very effective landing page you might consider having your ad as the 4th or 5th on the page. That way it's still fairly high but you won't have to pay too much per click. You can't command Google to put your ad in those spots. You have to manage that yourself by adjusting your bids for the keywords you're targeting.

1. You'll save money if you deselect "Display Network" under "Networks".

2. Enable Conversion Tracking.

3. Don't spread your resources too thin. Drop the keywords from your campaign that aren't working well, that is, that aren't getting clicks, people coming to your website.

4. Test continually. Test new ads that you've written, different variations of keywords, everything you can think of. Don't delete old ads, just pause them, so you can use them again later if you wish, or a version of them.

Google has a service called AdWords Express that will manage your AdWords advertising for you.

Managing your own pay per click advertising can take a lot of time, sometimes a number of hours every day. It's often better to hire an experienced company to do it for you that is Certified in Google AdWords. They will charge you a setup fee and a management fee.

The setup fee may be a month's budget. The management fee is usually between 15% and 25% of your monthly budget, but it's worth it. Unless you are an expert yourself, hiring an internet marketing company to manage them for you will make you money.

I. How To Make Any Word People Search For Show Up In Your Ad

Google AdWords and some other ad networks will let

you insert some code into your ads so that whatever keyword people search for appears in your ad. This is called Dynamic Keyword Insertion (DKI). You can also make it so their keywords appear in the display URL of your Landing Page in your ad. You can even make it so their keywords appear in the text on the Landing Page on your website.

It's an advanced feature of Google AdWords so it's not for beginners, but it's such a cool idea I wanted to show you that it's possible. If you want to find out more you can either search on Google for "AdWords Help DKI" or go to this URL - https://support.google.com/adwords/answer/74992?hl=en

J. The Power of Remarketing / Retargeting Pay Per Click Advertising

Google calls it Remarketing. Facebook calls it Retargeting. This is the service that will put a simple, harmless, plain text bit of code called a cookie on the computers of people who've been to your website. Then when they go to another website that has an agreement with Google, that website reads the cookie on their computer and shows them your ad.

It's proven to be a very powerful and profitable internet marketing method. It's more expensive than regular pay per click advertising but the return is usually much higher.

There are a number of well-established companies offering this service. They each offer their own version of Remarketing and have their own speciality and advantages. Some of them are AdRoll, Chango, Perfect Audience, Triggit, ReTargeter, and Google. You can choose Remarketing as an option right in your Google AdWords account.

K. Advantages of Building a Landing Page for Your Pay Per Click Ads

If you wish you can take people who click your ads to your homepage, but your pay per click advertising will make you more money if you take them to a page on your website that you've built especially for that purpose. This is called a Landing Page.

Google has a computer program that will look at your Landing Page and assess it. If it feels you have a good Landing Page they will display your ads higher up on their search results pages and charge you a lower cost per click. This means you'll save money and get more traffic to your website.

L. How to Build a Landing Page That Sells

There are millions of dollars spent every year on building and testing Landing Pages. It's quite a science, mostly to do with human behaviour and how to influence it with colors, shapes, text, etc. These are some of the basics:

1. It helps to put yourself in the shoes of a total stranger who has clicked your ad, and has come to your Landing Page for the first time. What is the first information they are looking for? What's the first question they want answered? Then what are they looking for? Try to follow the thought process of the visitor from start to finish, when you guide them to do what you want them to do.

2. Use the some of the same words and phrases in your Landing Page headlines and text as you did in your ad.

3. Everything on the page should either direct people to take the desired action, or reinforce

their decision to take the desired action. If there's something on the page that doesn't do that, remove it. You don't want to distract visitors. Help them keep their mind on what you want them to do. Don't even have links to the other pages on your website, or to other websites.

4. They've come to your website because they feel they have a problem. Talk about them and their problem, not about you.

5. Your text or short video should explain how your offer solves their problem, saves them from loss or gives them something they want but didn't have before.

6. The page layout should be easy to read.

7. Have a clear call to action, with a large colorful button that sticks out from the rest of the page.

8. It's powerful to talk about scarcity or a limited time offer, such as "only 7 widgets left" or "Sale ends Thursday".

9. Have your guarantee or trust signals right beside the button you want them to click to get your offer.

10. Make the button large, a different color than you've used on the page before so it sticks out, and the text on the button should not say "submit". It should say something like "Get my free widget now".

M. Can You Make Money With Google AdSense?

Any website can sign up to have Google pay per click ads on their website. This is called Google AdSense.

Every time a visitor to your website clicks a Google ad on your website you make a little money. If you have a lot of traffic to your website you can make a lot of money.

There was an article in the Vancouver Sun daily newspaper a few years ago talking about a local couple that was running a dating website called www.plentyoffish.com out of their apartment. They were making $300,000 a month from Google AdSense. But these situations are very rare. Most websites make very little.

It's free to sign up with Google for AdSense and there are no other costs. Google provides a tool that you can use to track your income. You choose where on your website the ads will be displayed, and what types of ads you will allow. Almost any kind of website can display Google AdSense ads.

The simple text ads are the most common, but you can have animated ads, video ads, and display ads of any size and shape. Google AdSense is most appropriate on websites that generate a great deal of visitors and aren't selling anything complicated or expensive.

We've included information here about Google AdSense only because we sometimes get questions about it. But we recommend against it. For a real estate agent or broker it is confusing for visitors to see ads on your website. They're not sure what the purpose of your website is, and It distracts them from your goal of getting them to contact you about real estate.

N. Pay-Per-Click Advertising On Other Major Websites

You can place your ads on other websites besides Google. For example, if you are advertising financial services you can ask Google to place your ads only on websites that offer financial services that aren't competing with your own. You can even select exactly which websites you want your ads to be on.

Many large websites with a lot of users have their own type of pay per click ads. Facebook, Twitter, Bing and LinkedIn also have their own pay per click ads. Google calls their pay per click ads "AdWords". Bing now calls their pay per click ads just "Bing Ads". Bing Ads run on both Bing and Yahoo. But both Bing and Yahoo have a very small percentage of the search market.

Google Adwords has been around the longest and is the most well-established. As a result, they are the most expensive pay-per-click ads. Other websites, such as Facebook, Twitter, and LinkedIn are not so well-established so their ads are less expensive on a cost per click basis.

1. **Facebook ads** – As just mentioned, Facebook ads are less expensive. They can also be targeted more closely to your target audience than Google AdWords. For example, on Facebook you can target your ads by location, gender, age, likes and interests, relationship status, workplace, and education. If you have a Facebook page you can target your ad to people who are already connected to you.

   Larger Facebook ads appear in people's desktop News Feed. Smaller Facebook ads appear in the right hand column of the page. You can have ads with images and even video on Facebook. Facebook has a large, easy to read section in their Help Center on how to run Facebook Ads. Some advertisers complain that the average age of Facebook users is increasing, but for real estate agents we see that as an advantage.

2. **Twitter ads** – Twitter also has a very comprehensive ad system with a well laid out and clearly worded Help Center. Twitter has a much smaller user base than Facebook but their users are generally more active. They're the segment of society that is more mobile, more affluent, and more into technology and leading-edge services.

3. **LinkedIn ads** – LinkedIn says it has the world's largest audience of active, influential professionals. You can target your ads by job title and function, by industry and company size, and by seniority. You can have text only ads, text and image ads, and video ads.

4. **Bing ads** – Bing ads are similar to Google AdWords except your cost per click will be significantly lower because their share of the search market is smaller. Their audience is smaller.

Conclusion

This chapter provided a general overview of most types of pay per click advertising, including the advantages and disadvantages compared to rankings in the organic, or not paid listings. We also discussed how to get started and several steps you can take to make it pay.

The next chapter talks about how to find a good internet marketing company. We also talk about how to avoid being ripped off, and how to work effectively with your internet marketing company.

JOIN OUR FREE WEBINAR AS A COMPANION TO THIS BOOK –

★ Register Now due to limited number of participants – Go to http://www.topagentinternetmarketing.com/FreeWebinar

"How Top Real Estate Agents are Using the Internet to Capture More Leads and Close More Sales"

- See more Real Life Examples

- Learn Advanced Strategies

- Watch the actual concepts and processes described in this book done for you live

- Qualify for a Free One-on-One Consultation ($500 value)

- Enter your name for a Free Website Analysis ($1,200 value)

CHAPTER 10
HOW TO FIND A GOOD INTERNET MARKETING COMPANY

© Randy Glasbergen
glasbergen.com

"Yes, I'm talking to a chocolate bar.
It doesn't have all the cool features of
a big phone, but it costs a lot less."

Any business person knows that no matter what you're buying you'll always be able to find something cheaper. But do you want something cheaper if it doesn't do what you need it to? How can it be just as good as the more expensive product or service?

I included this chapter because so many of our clients

say to me "Ken, I've dealt with three or four SEO companies in the past and never got anything from it until I
found Top Agent Internet Marketing".

I'm sorry to say there are a lot of Internet Marketing
companies out there who are more interested in getting
your money than delivering great value. As well there are
companies doing SEO who think they're doing it right and
don't understand why their clients are not getting results.

On top of that there are many website designers who,
when their clients ask them "Do you do SEO?" they say
"Yes." That's like asking your house painter if he builds
houses.

Designers like that don't realize they are hurting themselves in the long run, and they're hurting the whole industry. Every time someone doesn't get the results they expect
from their SEO provider people become more suspicious
of SEO work in general.

I'm including this chapter to encourage you, because
there's no need to feel helpless or frustrated. There are
a number of specific things you can watch out for when
choosing an SEO company, signs that they probably won't
give you the results you want. And there are also specific
signs you can look for that will give you a very good chance
of receiving an outstanding return on your investment.

A. Signs of Bad SEO Company

If you see any of these signs when looking for an SEO
company we recommend you look at them as harbingers of
trouble, quietly turn, and walk away.

1. **Secretive** - Beware of companies who won't
   explain what work they're doing on your website
   and your internet presence. It's true that some

parts of SEO are very technical, but all of these technical issues can be learned by any average person. So any average person can understand them if they're explained well. We're not doing brain surgery here.

2. **Too Much Jargon** - Beware of companies that throw jargon at you to try to make you feel stupid so you'll do whatever they say. If you don't understand what they're talking about, then ask them to explain it again. If they talk down to you, then they're not a good company. I've always said that if you can't explain what you're doing in simple language, you don't know what you're doing.

3. **SEO as a Sideline** - Beware of hiring companies whose main business is not SEO. There is so much new information for an SEO company to learn and incorporate into their systems all the time it absolutely requires a full time commitment, some would even say more than a full time commitment. There are usually many long days required in the SEO business.

As well, so many of the most important things we've learned about making money for our clients we've learned by doing, by not listening to Google or what anybody else says, by finding out what works and what doesn't in the real world for our specific customers. That kind of experience comes only when you're up to your eyeballs in SEO for real estate agents every day for many years.

4. **SEO by the Keyword** - Some SEO companies will "sell you a keyword". What?!! That's abso-

lutely ridiculous. Some pay per click advertising could possibly be packaged for sale that way. But we wouldn't recommend it even for that, and particularly not for Organic Search Engine Optimization.

The reason is that Google is so good at giving high rankings to websites that are an authority in their field that once your website is ranking well for one keyword phrase in that field it will automatically rank well for many keyword phrases in that field.

Another reason why it's not productive to do SEO by the keyword is that Google has become very good these days at Semantic Indexing. "Indexing" just means that when they scan your website they give your content labels, so when they save it into their memory banks they can easily find it when they want it.

"Semantic" just means that their computer program that scans your website is very good at understanding the "gist" of what the text says, the general meaning of what it's talking about.

Google's is so good at Semantic Indexing that you almost don't need to include keywords in your webpage content anymore. For small real estate websites it's good to include it in some of the URL's of the pages, the Title Tags, in the H1 Tags, and once in the body text of pages. But other than that, if you simply write your content for people rather than for search engines, Google's ranking algorithm will know what you're talking about just fine.

B. Signs of a Good SEO Company

As an insider in the SEO industry I can tell you that there are a number of signals that indicate the probability of a satisfactory long term relationship with a particular company is high.

1. **In SEO for 10 Years or More** – I've mentioned before that there have been so many changes to Google's ranking criteria in the last 10 years it would be very difficult to understand them all and get good rankings for your clients unless you'd been in the business during that time.

2. **SEO is their Main Business** – I also mentioned that SEO demands so much time and so many resources just to keep up with all the changes, that you must be involved in it on a full time basis. Perhaps more importantly, you need to be doing it every day for a long time in order to see what works in the real world for your clients regardless of what anybody else says.

3. **Specialize in Your Industry** – It's common sense that the more you do something the better you get. If the SEO company you hire is working specializing in clients in real estate sales it's logical they will be better at it than a company who isn't.

4. **Work with Small Clients** – If an SEO company hasn't worked with small businesses for a long time they wouldn't understand that Google's criteria for giving websites high rankings can be very different for small websites than for large websites depending on the situation.

5. **Speak So You Understand** – If the SEO company

you're working with won't take the time to explain what they're doing, or if they can't explain it in terms you can understand, then either they don't know what they're doing or they don't have a good attitude toward customer service.

C. Questions to Ask Before You Commit

The most important thing I can say here is that you need to find a company you can trust. That's the crucial ingredient in any relationship. If you don't trust them, then don't work with them. If you trust them, then try to take their advice and let them do their job.

But even if you trust them it's good to ask questions. You need to go into any new relationship with your eyes open.

1. **What They Will Be Doing** – Don't be afraid to ask what work they'll be doing on your website, your blog, your social media accounts, and your backlinks. If they don't answer this question to your satisfaction how can you trust them?

2. **Length of Commitment** - Ask how long you need to commit for. Most SEO companies require a 12 month commitment. You have to understand that good SEO will turn your website from an expense into a profit center, but it won't happen overnight. Google takes its time.

3. **Time Until Return On Investment** - Ask how long it will take before your investment starts bringing a return. Three to six months before you start getting leads is normal, unless your situation has special challenges, in which case it could be eight to twelve months. If you're not prepared to

wait that long, or if you can't afford it at this time, then it's better to wait until you are ready.

4. **How Much Return** – Ask what kind of Return on Investment you can expect. The more you invest the greater return you can expect.

5. **Pricing** – Understand that if they are good they won't be cheap. So much work has to be done every month to show Google your website is an authority in your area, and that it's up to date. You will always be able to find somebody who will work for less, but will they do the same quality of work, and the same amount of work? How can they.

6. **Payments** – Is there a large setup fee, or are payments the same every month?

7. **Extra Costs** - Ask if there are any other costs besides SEO? They may offer optional services such as website design, video production or podcast production.

D. How to Work with Your SEO Company

Good management of the beginning of a relationship sets the stage for long term benefit. Once you've found an SEO company you can trust it will help to form a good working relationship. People do better work when they're happy. And it's easier to be happy if everybody knows what's expected of them.

Think about the kind of clients you want to work with, and try to be one of those. Here are some tips that may help:

1. **Grow With You** - SEO is something you'll always

need. If you jump from company to company, each new company will need to spend some time and probably take some of your time, to learn about your strengths and your goals, formulate a plan, and take the action required to get things started. It's more cost effective if you find a company that plans to grow with you so you only have to go through that process once.

2. **Positive** - Approach the relationship with a positive attitude. If you can't be optimistic it won't work. After you've found somebody you can trust don't shop around for SEO advice. Don't second guess them. If you hear about something new and are wondering if it would help your website, don't demand they do it for you, ask them about it. Use them as your ongoing Internet Marketing Consultants.

3. **Ask About Their Plan** - Ask your SEO company what their plan is to increase the qualified traffic to your website, and to increase the leads you receive from it. If you have questions or concerns about their plan ask right at the beginning of your relationship, not down the road when the plan is already in place. Once the plan is in place be prepared to stick to it.

4. **Limited Responsibility** - Understand you only hired them to increase the traffic to your website and the leads you receive from it. They are not responsible if your computer isn't working and you can't see your website, or if you are having problems with your email. You have to hire a local

computer technical support company to solve those problems.

E. Frustrated and Overwhelmed?

In this book I haven't held anything back. I've done my best to give it all away. If you want to do it yourself I wish you nothing but the best. It is possible. Most of our clients feel they'll make more money by selling real estate, and letting us manage their SEO but that's entirely up to you. If you wish we can do it all for you.

If you're thinking about working with another SEO company you can use this book as a guide so you'll understand what they're doing and why.

If you're thinking about working with us I can tell you that although we are very busy we do accept new clients from time to time. We are not a large company. We're a boutique firm. And we can only take a certain number of clients in each major market because there are only so many spots at the top of page one of Google.

Some things to know before you call us:

1. We work only with serious business people who want to do significantly more ends next year, make more money, have more time off, and enjoy a profitable and stress-free business.

2. Our service is not cheap. Our clients tell us they would rather pay a little more and receive a good return on their investment than pay a little less and get nothing.

3. SEO is our only business. We make world-class websites only because it's such an important part of SEO.

4. We build only custom WordPress websites. Website design costs are extra but it's a one-time cost, and it's entirely optional. We can usually work with your existing website. If we can't we'll tell you.

5. If we build you a website you'll still be a client of a company that provides MLS® System IDX. We'll install it on your website and make sure everything works properly. We can often recommend a good IDX supplier depending on your location. You'll have to contact them yourself and set up your account. It's quick and easy, usually only $50 or $60 a month.

6. If you want video and/or podcast production for your website those costs are extra. We can help you with that if you wish to ensure all of your marketing pieces are consistent with your brand. Or you can have someone else produce them and we'll put them on your website.

7. We accept payment by credit card only. We accept payments from your credit card on the 25th of each month for the following month.

8. We require a 12 month commitment. It takes a number of months for Google to recognize your website as an authority, so a commitment of less than 12 months is not giving yourself a fair chance to reap the benefits. After the first year most clients continue on a month to month basis.

9. Your minimum monthly payments will be the same every month. You can increase your budget any time you want more leads.

10. We've been in business since 1999.

11. We work exclusively with real estate agents and brokers.

12. We're Certified by Google in AdWords, their Pay Per Click advertising system.

13. We're also Certified by Google in Analytics, their system for reporting statistics about the people who come to your website.

14. We don't outsource SEO work to Asia. We do it all in-house. That's the only way we can know exactly what's going on and maintain the highest quality for every client.

If you're interested in doing business with us you can call and ask for me - Ken Lapp. I'll talk to you personally. I'm the President of Top Agent Internet Marketing. If I'm not available at the time it's only because we're very busy. Leave a message and I'll return your call as soon as I can.

F. Bonus Chapters

We've included four bonus chapters after this one with more in-depth information on important SEO related issues. Please enjoy them.

Bonus Chapter 1 - Social Media For Real Estate Agents

Bonus Chapter 2 - Blogging For Profit

Bonus Chapter 3 - All About Online Reviews

Bonus Chapter 4 - Google My Business

G. Feedback

I'd like to hear your feedback. If you've taken the time to read this book you're a person with above average determination who is dedicated to their success. You are the type of person I most like to hear from. You could tell me what you liked about the book, what you didn't like about it, what other topics you would like me to include if I do a second edition, or anything else.

Please go to http://www.topagentinternetmarketing. com/SOLD/bookfeedback and let me know your thoughts. Thank you.

Ken Lapp

BONUS CHAPTER 1
SOCIAL MEDIA FOR REAL ESTATE AGENTS

AFTER ALL OUR ONLINE CHATS, I'M HAPPY TO FINALLY MEET YOU IN PERSON!

ME TOO!

© Randy Glasbergen / glasbergen.com

Some real estate agents spend time on Social Media because they don't like to meet people in person. But if you use it as a way to set up in-person meetings with friends and family of clients Social Media can be an important part of your business. It can expand your sphere of influence, develop trust and get people talking about you.

The first section here contains specific suggestions on how to use seven of the most popular social media websites. The second section talks about general social media guidelines.

A. Tips on Using the 7 of the Most Important Social Media Websites

You don't have to be active on all of these social media websites. Choose one or two, become active, and see how much time you have left.

There is a great deal to learn about using each of these social media websites well. Here are a few suggestions for ways real estate agents can use them.

1. **Google+** (pronounced 'Google Plus')
   This is the social media website started by Google. It has never been well used but it's very important from an SEO point of view because of the verification processes involved, and because it's owned by Google.

   1) This is a mandatory social media account for every real estate agent with a website, due to the verification process. It helps Google rank your website properly and more quickly.

   2) Google will rank your website higher whenever anyone in your Google+ network searches on Google or in Google+, if that person is logged in to their Google account. Many people are logged into their Google account all the time so they can easily check their email on Gmail. So it pays to have a large Google+ network, that is, many people in your circles.

   3) Some experts say Google will rank your posts on Google+ higher and for longer than posts on your other social media accounts.

2. Facebook

In the first quarter of 2015 Facebook had 1.44 billion monthly active users. It's great for expressing yourself in photos and text, for connecting with people who have similar interests, and for marketing your personal brand. It's good for real estate agents because older demographics are using it more and more.

1) Don't use your personal Facebook page. It's better to set up a page for your business.

2) Show interesting photos of your neighbourhood or area of specialization. Show your passion for your area and your knowledge of it.

3) Post about local events in your area. If you're going to attend, invite them to meet you there.

4) Facebook lets you target ads very specifically. You can use "Promoted Posts" very inexpensively to attract interest for events in your area.

5) You might post a photo of you elegantly welcoming a client to their new home on possession day.

6) The rule in social media is to make 80% of your posts about things other than yourself, such as your area of specialization or something new in the industry, and 20% about you and your listings.

7) You can use hashtags, for example "#kitsilano" or "#staging", but you'll only see posts that were shared with you.

8) You can have contests and giveaways to encourage interaction with your Facebook page. For example, you could have a photo contest for shots of your neighbourhood. You need a third party app.

9) If you post a photo it's good to tag the people who are in the photo with you, so the photo can show up on their timeline.

3. **Twitter**

In the first quarter of 2105 Twitter had 236 million monthly active users. Twitter is used for short messages, 140 characters or less. It's quick, and used more by tech savvy people and business people who want to know what's happening right now. It's most famous for people tweeting their thoughts while they're in the middle of an event.

1) Twitter is a great social media platform for news and events, even small news about your neighborhood and events in it.

2) It can be good to tweet helpful tips about Staging or Moving.

3) Using hashtags in your tweets will mean your tweets are seen by more than just your followers. They will be seen by people searching for those terms as well.

4) Using @mentions helps the person or company you're mentioning because it gives them free publicity. It helps establish you as a giver.

5) You can tweet about your listings if you use the 80/20 rule.

6) You can ask questions, for example, what's the best thing about living in (your area of specialization).

7) You can have contests and giveaways.

4. **Instagram**

Instagram has 300 million active users per month. It is the fastest growing social media website. It's focused on photos and images. When it started it was exclusively for mobile users, but recently they've made it so you can create your Web Profile including your Bio. Instagram was bought by Facebook in April 2012, so you can easily share your photos on Facebook.

1) It's good to show a 'behind the scenes' look at the steps you take to prepare one of your listings before a showing.

2) Some experts say a photo will stay at the top of people's news feeds if you post it to Facebook through Instagram.

3) On Instagram you can make a nice looking and interesting "Photo Map" of your neighbourhood showing where every photo was taken, businesses you've been to, events you've attended. This proves you are an expert in that area.

4) Include a link to your website in your Instagram Bio.

5) You can upload a 15 second video tour of one of your listings.

5. Pinterest

Pinterest has 50 million active users per month. It's the fourth largest social media website. Pinterest is also about connection through pictures and images.

1) It's good to set up a Board about your area of specialization, points of interest, seasonal shots, local businesses, amenities.

2) It can be good to further establish your personal brand by showing yourself getting involved in the community. You can talk about your hobbies, location of local tennis courts, anything you have passion for. It helps people get to know you.

3) You can also set up Board for your listings.

4) You can also use contests and giveaways here, for example, a video contest about your area of specialization.

5) You can have a Pinterest Tab on your Facebook page, where you get Pinterest updates.

6. LinkedIn

LinkedIn has a more mature membership, and sometimes more affluent. You can often communicate directly with CEO's of companies that you would otherwise have a hard time reaching, and finding something in common.

1) Write a good summary of yourself and why it's good to deal with you for selling and buying.

2) Show your passion for your area of specialization.

3) Good to join local groups and participate in them. Remember to establish yourself as a giver before you start promoting yourself.

7. **YouTube**

YouTube boasts 1 billion active users per month. That is almost half of the world's internet users. When you upload your videos to YouTube they will give you a short piece of embed code that you can insert into one of the pages on your website, so your video will play on your web page.

1) Great for having an intro video about yourself on your website so strangers can get to know you and learn how you feel about your area of specialization.

2) Of course it's also great for videos of your area.

3) You can have a video for each of your listings if you wish, and post them on your website.

B. 9 Social Media Guidelines and Best Practices

1. **Brand It**

When possible, avoid the default look of your chosen Social Networks when setting up your profile. Use your logo and any brand identifiers that you can. This includes background images, profile pictures, taglines and more. Try to ensure your entire social presence on all your social media accounts is well branded, professional and consistent. This will help the general public and your followers recognize you better, and it also reflects a higher level of professionalism.

2. **Be Socially Proactive**

Follow and "like" others first and they will usually reciprocate. It's important to join existing conversations, but remember social media is just like any other social setting you've ever been to, like walking into a party where you don't know anybody. You want to create conversation with people, not yell at them or talk about yourself all the time, or talk so much they can't share their own opinions.

3. **Know Who to Follow/Like**

Many real estate agents pack their Social Media networks with other real estate agents. While that can be good, it's important to follow current customers, past customers, and potential customers.

When users you don't know interact with your content make sure to acknowledge them with a Thank You, tag them in your reply, and follow them. This is a tried and true way of expanding your network and attracting more traffic to your social profiles and website.

4. **Show Personality**

Link Dropping is when you include a link in your social media content without saying anything about where the link will take users. It's about the same as copying a bunch of links to articles and pasting them all over your social networks. People don't respond to link dropping because they don't know where the link goes, how it relates to them and what's in it for them. When you share a link make sure you introduce the article and let your followers know why they should click it.

It's also recommended that you choose specific interests to share with your networks. These interests can be related to your area of specialization or not, but they should be something you and your team knows something about. Sharing emerging artists, trending photography and promotions for concerts, and gallery shows you are interested in the arts and culture.

5. **Create Content**

   Create content for your website that can be referred to on your Social Media accounts. It's best if you can use information valuable to your social media fans/followers so they will return to your social media page.

   Blogs posts, photos, videos, and/or shared articles about what's new in the real estate industry or in your neighbourhood are great ways to keep your accounts active. It's best if you can introduce your content in a way that your followers can make a connection. If you share a photo make sure to include a little back story on what was going on when the photo was taken or why the photo is interesting.

6. **Interact**

   Don't hesitate to like, share, +1, or retweet other people's content that you appreciate or agree with. Paying attention to what your followers and networks are talking about is a part of market research, and it's good to stay on top of trending topics. This could help you form ideas for your next tweet or other project. Interacting with your network is a good way to increase engagement with your social media accounts and your website, and will lead to more likes for you.

7. **Keep Current**
Update your accounts regularly - daily is best, or just as often as you can. If you find yourself completely stumped about what content to post on a particular day, simply mentioning something you are grateful for can go a long way in developing your brand online.

Pay attention to local news, industry news, and national and international news, as these all present opportunities for sharing trending stories. Staying on top of world events is a good way to "newsjack" a story (hijack a news story) and be the first to inform your network of the event. Also, keeping on top of industry news is a good way to establish youself as an authority figure in the industry.

Staying on top of trending topics is a good way to develop common ground with your followers. However, exercise caution as you want to maintain a level of professionalism and branding. Some trending topics won't be relevant to your industry or your followers, and sharing content like this may reflect poorly on your brand.

8. **Schedule**
You don't have to spend time on Social Media every day to maintain your brand's presence on a daily basis. There are fantastic free software options, such as HootSuite, that allow you to pre-schedule

tweets and Facebook posts days, weeks, or months in advance.

However, solely relying on HootSuite is not recommended as you miss out on a lot of content shared by your network, and if you never interact with your network how will you build a trusting and loyal following? It's best to use a mix of scheduling posts and actually visiting each social media website to interact with your network and see what they're sharing.

Also, if there is a catastrophe or international event you'll have to pause your prescheduled content releases or risk coming off as callous and uninformed.

9. **Link Back to Your Website**

Your website is the foundation of all your Internet Marketing, and Social Media Networks are just the icing on the cake. While it is possible to get leads from Social Media accounts directly it's usually better to bring people back to your website. There you have the opportunity to educate them, convince them, and get them to contact you.

If you post an interesting blog to your social media it's good to ensure people can visit your website to "learn more" about whatever your post was about.

BONUS CHAPTER 2
BLOGGING FOR PROFIT

GLASBERGEN
© Randy Glasbergen
glasbergen.com

"I realized I have too many high-tech gadgets
when I became Facebook friends with my toaster."

It could be said that blogging is the least technical Social
Media activity you can do. It's part of Social Media
because readers can respond directly to any of your blog
articles.

Please see the Introduction to this book for an explanation of basic blogging terminology. It can be very confusing.

The most important thing about blogging is that we

have seen a direct relationship between active blogs and high rankings in Google. A blog that has a lot of high quality content, and is constantly adding content makes your website more of an authority. And of course Google wants to give high rankings to websites that are an authority in their field.

At a minimum your blog will help your rankings on Google and build traffic to your website. We literally write hundreds of high quality original content blog articles for our clients every month.

However, if you want to write additional blogs of your own, over time your blog can build to become the most powerful online marketing tool you've ever had. And best of all it's completely free. All it takes is some time and a bit of inspiration. This bonus chapter is designed to help you with that inspiration, and to make your blogging as easy and as productive as possible.

At its best a well-constructed, regularly updated blog can transform your website into a hub for your industry. But even if your blog is not the center of your industry blogging can really be fun. In return for a few minutes a week you get to:

- Air your opinions

- Demonstrate your knowledge and expertise

- Create a bond of trust between you and potential customers

- Build a larger network and increase social media presence

- Drive more traffic to your website

- Improve your rankings on Google

A. What Not To Do

Before we tell you what to do we want to help you avoid the serious problems you can get into by blogging the wrong way:

1) **Duplicate Content** – Google doesn't like it if you copy articles or information from another website and put it on your website. The don't even like it if you copy content from your own pages and put it on other pages of your website.

2) **Keyword Stuffing** – If you include your keywords in your blog articles too often Google will penalize your rankings. Don't write articles for rankings. Write articles for your readers. It's good to include your keyword in the title and once in the content. More than that is not necessary, and may lower your rankings.

3) **External Links** – It's better for your rankings if you don't have links to other websites on your blogs, and actually on the rest of your website pages as well. Another reason not to do that is that the goal is always to keep visitors on your website for as long as possible. It's better not to make it too easy or attractive for them to leave.

4) **New Listings and Opens** - Simply adding your open houses and new listings to your blog is not an effective use of a blog in Google's eyes. We recommend not to do it. Better to have a separate page on your website called "Open Houses" if you wish, and a page for your individual listings.

B. How to Avoid Problems Writing Your Blogs

Before you start writing there may be some challenges to your creativity. Don't let them get in your way. The trick is to acknowledge these challenges and understand that even the best writers have writers block sometimes. So let's put these challenges on the table and expose them for what they are:

1) **The "I can't" attitude** - We encourage you to just write anything that comes into your head, and then go over it and edit it until you're OK with putting it on your website. This is a very common method among professional writers.

2) **The perfectionist** - Perfection doesn't exist, so give it your best shot and we can assure you that your writing will improve over time. 80% is good enough. Get it done and out the door. Some action, any action, is better than waiting for perfection.

3) **The concern of making a mistake in your facts** - Remember what we said above, no one is perfect. Everybody makes mistakes. It's quite common for readers to correct writers – and that's okay! So do your homework and try to get your facts right, but don't worry about it if you're not always right. Something you can do to make yourself look good is to include a link in your blog to the webpage where you got your information.

4) **The worry of no one reading it** - Sure, you may not get as many readers on your first blog post as your 20th or 50th. But like most

things, the more you put into it, the more momentum you'll build up, and the better you'll get. The response you receive will increase over time.

5) **The lack of originality** - As Pablo Picasso said "Good artists copy; great artists steal." Ideas are free – so read relevant blogs for ideas and add your personality. You can write on any topic as long as you do it in your own words. Using other people's exact words is plagiarism. It will get you in trouble.

C. 24 Guidelines for Writing Great Blog Articles

1) **Every Blog** – There are a number of things every blog article you post on your blog should have:

    a. Although you don't want to use keywords too many times, Google still has to know what the blog is about. So it's good to have a keyword in the title, in the Meta Description Tag, and perhaps once or twice in the text.

    b. A relevant photo to make it more interesting to the reader. You can buy stock photos for a few dollars from websites like StockFresh, Fotolia, and iStockphoto.

    c. A link in the text to another page on your website that talks about a similar issue.

    d. Social media icons at the bottom so readers can share the article with their network if they wish.

e. A call-to-action, even if it's just a gentle suggestion they contact you for more information with a link to your "Contact Me" page.

f. A small form where they can sign up to receive the RSS feed for your blog. That way they can automatically receive every blog article you post either in their RSS reader, or by email.

2) **Local Events** – One of the best things to write about in your blog is events that are happening in your neighbourhood. It could be a Farmer's Market, Craft Fair, Rummage Sale, Parade, dances, plays. All of those make timely and interesting reading for your prospects.

3) **More Information** – You can write in greater detail about a new listing. If you specialize in an area it's good to build up the local attractions, parks, trails, tennis courts, etc. This is your chance to show people that you care and provide them with information they won't get from your competitors.

4) **Solve Customer Problems** – This is another important thing you can do with your blog. It will help build traffic and rankings because people are probably searching on Google for answers to their problems. Think of the questions your customers ask, and write your answers.

5) **Friendly** - Blogs work best if they're helpful,

entertaining and personal. Write your blog like you are speaking to a single reader and express yourself informally like you would to a friend over coffee, giving your personal opinions as well as your professional ideas.

6) **Outrageous** - It's actually good to be a little outrageous, as long as you don't alienate your potential customers or hurt your image. It's much easier to get noticed if you are different.

7) **Authors** - If more than one person is going to be writing on your blog make sure they each have their own user name so readers can see who is writing and can feel connected to each person.

8) **Length** - In terms of length, there are no absolute rules. But if you use too many redundant words people will get bored and leave. Just make sure you use enough words to explain your point fully. If you only need 50 words use 50 words. For Search Engine Optimization (SEO) the longer the better.

9) **Single Topic** – It's best to write a separate blog article for each different topic. Otherwise readers get confused. If you find yourself going off on a tangent save the thought, copy it into a new document, and use it as the basis for your next blog post.

10) **Stories** - People love stories, so try to think of things that have happened in your business or personal life and use them as a starting point. Ask colleagues if they have a funny story

about their day at work or an unusual situation they found themselves in.

11) **Real Estate Issues** - You know what's important to your potential clients, so put that information on your blog. News is free. You can re-write stories you find in the newspapers or see on TV in your own words and add your feelings to them. Subscribe to the important real estate blogs or journals. You can find them just by searching on Google for topics related to your industry.

For example, if you are a real estate agent in Edmonton, subscribe to the Alberta government's monthly economic review, pull out information about home sales and interest rate trends, then write about how this might help or hinder the home buyers you deal with every day.

12) **Regular** - Blogs should be kept up to date. Once a week is a good minimum, but just do what you can. Something is better than nothing. Post your blog articles at the same time of day on the same day of the week on a regular basis, so readers know when to expect the next article.

13) **Writing / Publishing** - Set aside a few minutes three times a week to write your blogs. When you get ideas for a new post jot them down on a piece of paper. Write several blog posts at one time. Head to your favourite coffee shop, give yourself three hours, and try to write five or six blog posts. Publish them one

at a time over the next five or six weeks.

14) **Celebrity Guest Bloggers** - Invite big names in your area, including important bloggers, to write posts on your blog. A lot of them will want the publicity so they'll be happy to do it. They might promote your blog on their blog if you suggest it.

15) **Social Media** – After you've established yourself as a giver on your social media networks, that is, someone interested not just in promoting themselves but in helping others, it's good once in a while to share a link to one of the blog posts on your website on the topic being discussed.

16) **Promote Others** - Your blog is a good place to promote others, such as the service providers in your referral network, plumbers, landscapers, etc. They may help to promote you in return, as well as referring clients to you.

17) **Suppliers** – Or you could ask them if they want to write an article for your blog on their products and services. The might be happy to have the opportunity for free exposure. You can tone it down if it turns out to be a 500 word commercial.

18) **Perspective** – It can be good to interview somebody important in real estate in your area, or even somebody who has seen the changes over the years.

19) **Jargon** – It can be good to help prospects un-

derstand the language used in your industry.

20) **Question** – It can be good to start off with a question to get people thinking and mentally engaged in the article. The first sentence is the key to generating enough interest in reading the entire article.

21) **Skimmers** - Format the text in your blog post for skimmers, using many headings, bullet points, and occasional bold text for important points.

22) **Specific Numbers** – It's good to open your blog article with industry research and studies. People want to know specific facts. People are also more likely to share articles that introduce and discuss interesting research and relevant facts.

23) **Quotes** - Using quotes and block quotes is a great way to add some credibility and support to your claims and opinions. It's always good to include the source of your information.

24) **CoSchedule** - For $10 a month you can use a good WordPress plugin called CoSchedule that will automatically post your bogs to your social media accounts. It's better to write different entries on your social media accounts, but publishing your blog posts automatically is better than nothing.

BONUS CHAPTER 3
HOW TO GET VALUABLE ONLINE REVIEWS, AND DEAL WITH TROUBLE MAKERS

REAL
ESTATE

© Randy Glasbergen / glasbergen.com

GLASBERGEN

"This house has a great location! If you own a really good pair of shoes, it's within walking distance of Disneyland, Cape Cod, the Grand Canyon, Mall of America, and Carnegie Hall!"

To get good reviews as a real estate agent you have to be careful not to exaggerate. You have to be friendly and professional. You have to be constantly thinking about each clients' needs. You have to be honest even when you think nobody will ever find out.

This bonus chapter talks about why reviews are

important for your business, how to encourage clients to give you positive reviews, and what to do if you receive negative reviews.

A. Why Online Reviews Are So Important

One reason online reviews are important is that "social proof" is becoming more important. Social proof means as human beings we are looking for proof others have been happy dealing with a particular business or real estate agent, for example. Testimonials are a kind of social proof. Reviews are another.

We believe if many others have decided it's good to do something, eat at a particular restaurant or deal with a particular real estate agent, for example, then it's a good indication it would be good for us as well. Online reviews are one way to show complete strangers they can trust you.

Another reason they're important is that positive online reviews affect your Google rankings. As with so many things about Google's ranking criteria there is no definitive proof. However, there is a lot of evidence to indicate Google takes it as a positive signal.

B. Don't Fake It

Because reviews influence prospects there is an increasing amount of fake reviews appearing on review websites. It has grown into such a problem that the State of New York is collaborating with businesses to curb deception and punish those that post fake reviews. Eric T. Schneiderman, the New York attorney general, called fake reviews "worse than old-fashioned false advertising."

Most review websites rate businesses with a star system. If you have more stars it means you have more positive reviews. In a 2011 study, Harvard Business School discovered restaurants that improved their ranking by just one star, increased their revenue up to 9 percent. Even though the benefits are tempting we highly recommended businesses do not partake in submitting fake reviews. The results of getting caught can be disastrous.

C. Doing It Right

There are some rules you should keep in mind while working on building up your reviews:

1) **No incentivizing reviews** - You can't offer discounts or giveaways in exchange for reviews.

2) **Should be natural** - You can't have a computer or tablet in your office for facilitating reviews. This is because Yelp, Google, and other review based websites track the IP addresses of each computer that submits a review. If too many reviews are submitted from the same computer the website will block that computer.

3) **Filters for the Over Enthusiastic** - Review websites have filters in place for blocking reviews that seem overly enthusiastic.

D. How to Get More Valuable Reviews

1) **Provide Instructions** – Once you are sure a customer is happy with your service you could email them complete instructions on how to submit a review on each of the main review websites. It's good to make it as easy as possible. This helps to encourage variety in review websites, which make your reviews look more natural.

2) **Ask at the Best Time** – It's better to ask for a

review when people have just received some good news.

3) **Advertise With Signage** - Placing a simple Yelp or Google Reviews sticker somewhere where clients will see it will help introduce that fact that you welcome reviews.

4) **Display Old Reviews** - Print either your favorite or old reviews on your website, your brochure, and presentation materials.

5) **Include Reviews on Your Social Media** - Publicly thanking your customers via social media is a good way to show appreciation to those that took the time to review your service. It also provides the opportunity to showcase your review.

6) **Don't Have Big Expectations** – Building up your reviews takes time so don't get upset if they don't come in as fast as you'd like. Focus on wowing your customers and eventually they will be sure to give you reviews.

E. How To Deal With Trouble Makers

If positive reviews help your Google rankings it's also likely that negative reviews hurt your rankings. This issue is particularly important because there is nothing to stop an unscrupulous competitor from giving you a negative review. Negative reviews can be very difficult or impossible to get rid of.

There are a number of things to say about negative reviews. The first is that a bona fide negative review can actually help your credibility if you handle the situation well. Most people realize that there are always going to be a few unhappy and unreasonable people out there, and that these are the people who make the most noise.

There is a school of thought that says negative reviews are usually made by unhappy, unreasonable people. So if you go out of your way, go to any extent to turn them into a happy customer, they will turn into one of your greatest boosters, because they're not used to being treated that way. Everyone else treats them the way they deserve, badly. If you treat them well they will be so happy about it they will tell everybody they can.

These are a few suggestions on how to turn a bona fide negative review into a positive situation for you or your team, or at least mitigate the damage:

1) **Respond Quickly** – Instantly is best. For this reason it's good to have some software monitoring mentions of you or your team on the internet. You can use Google Alerts. It's free and very good for the price. But for better monitoring that saves you time you may want to pay a monthly fee or buy other software. There are a number of solutions available.

2) **Take It Off-line** – Minimize the negatives about you online by taking it offline as soon as possible. If you know who the complainer is call them on the phone immediately and ask to meet. A public place is usually best. It's good to take someone with you as a witness. They never say anything, just listen.

3) **Anonymous** – If they won't identify themselves just type something as a response, such

as "We would like very much to resolve this situation as soon as possible, but I hope you can understand that until we know who we're dealing with we can't take the issue seriously."

4) **Be Professional** – This is very important. You have to be absolutely detached and professional. If you react to their unfair criticism with any kind of emotion at all, you lose. Be positive, say nice things about them, assume they are a pleasant, reasonable, and logical person. Explain the facts. Deal only with the facts, no matter what they say or do.

5) **Apologize** – Usually what people want is an apology. We recommend you do it even if you feel you didn't do anything wrong. Do it because it will help your reputation and your business. Perhaps you could say something like "Although I don't feel there was anything I could have done to avoid this situation I'm sorry things didn't go as you wanted them to." You are not admitting guilt. You are saying you are sorry they are upset.

6) **Admit Guilt If Guilty** – If you or one of your team is guilty admit it immediately. Explain it was a mistake and what you've done to ensure it won't happen again. Explain what you're going to do to rectify the situation, and make them happy.

7) **Give Them Whatever They Want** – You may have to ask directly what they want. Even if what they're asking for is completely out of

line with what happened, give in. This may
be a tough thing to do, but we highly recommend it. It's worth it to avoid the trouble to
your business in the future. The only caveat I
would mention is, as long as they aren't asking
you to look worse in public or on the internet.
A negative review can haunt you and hurt your business for years. It's always better to resolve it quickly and
completely no matter how small it seems at the time.

BONUS CHAPTER 4
THE INCREDIBLE POWER OF A FREE GOOGLE MY BUSINESS ACCOUNT

"This home has a wonderful view. If you go outside at night, you can look up and see the whole universe!"

I couldn't think of a way to tie this cartoon in with this chapter. I just thought it was funny. ☺

So, to the point. Google knows that most of the commerce in the world is conducted by small local businesses. So they created Google My Business (formally known as Google+ Local, and before that as Google Places) to give local business owners the opportunity to get on Google search results for free.

The idea is that once local business owners get used to being on the internet, and start getting prospects and leads they'll want to get more. Then they will spend their money on AdWords, Google's pay per click advertising.

Google My Business helps consumers find, interact with, and review businesses in their own local neighborhood. This is accomplished by combining Google Maps and the Google+ community.

This means one thing – you need to get on the Google Map and optimize your Google+ presence by setting-up your Google My Business profile. Every real estate agent should have their own free Google My Business account.

This bonus chapter will help you connect with customers searching for you locally in your area of specialization. With our easy-to-follow steps you'll be able to setup a Google+ personal profile, optimize your Google My Business page, and be found on Google.

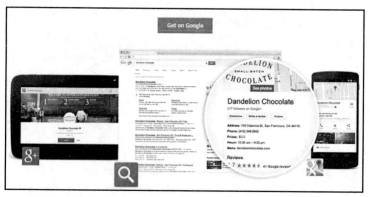

A. What is Google My Business?

Google+ internet properties have over *540 million active monthly users, including 300 million active monthly users on Google+ itself. Google My Business makes it possible to reach these users, your local customers, and have them interact with you through *their own* Google+ account. The Google+ Local tab in a user's Google+ profile allows them to discover local businesses that their network of followers in their Google+ Circles have visited and/or done business with. Users then return to Google+ account to write reviews, +1 posts related to their recent purchase, and engage others in discussions around their experience with those businesses.

Most importantly, the browsing and search history of a user is recorded by Google+. This increases the likelihood that they and their entire network will come across your business when they search on Google from then on.

It's imperative that every real estate agent set up and optimize their Google My Business profile so they can attract these potential customers.

Source: MarketingLand

B. Google Reviews

As soon as you've set-up your Google My Business profile, satisfied customers can find you using their Google+ Local tab, write a review, and rate your local business using the five star system.

Followers of these users will see these positive reviews in their Google+ news feed.

In addition, the more positive reviews you receive through the consumer driven Google+ Local system, the more likely your business will move ahead of your competition on Google search results, especially when searchers are signed into their Google accounts.

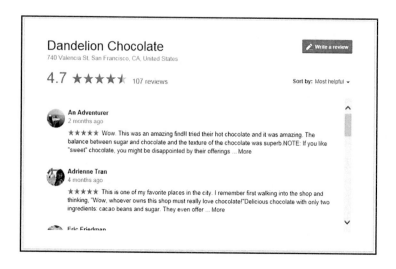

C. Google+ Circles

a. How to Look at Circles as a Business

To you, as a local business, Circles are defined as the groups of individuals, businesses, or organizations that interact with you through Google+. You can have Circles for *Customers*, *VIPs*, *Team Members*, a generic *Following*, and you can even customize your Circles using keywords to identify them.

b. How Your Customers Look at Circles

To the public, your customers, Circles are defined as the people who interact with them through Google+. They can have Circles for *Friends*, *Family*, *Acquaintances*, *Following*, and customized Circles. When they post a review about your business through Google+ this review becomes visible to all of the people in their Circles. So putting time into building your Circles with relevant and nearby people can be a great way to get free advertising.

D. Checklist for an Optimized Google My Business Profile

David Mihm from Moz.com published the results of the Local Search Ranking Factors Survey for 2014. http://moz.com/local-search-ranking-factors

This is a compilation of the best guesses of a number of companies in the Search Engine Optimization industry about the factors that influence the rankings on Google of your Google My Business listing, in order of importance.

1. **On-page Signals** - 21%
   The clear presence of your NAP(Name, Address, Phone) on your website, keywords or related words in website page titles and content, high domain authority.

2. **Link Signals** - 18.3%
   Quality and quantity of links on other websites that are pointing to your website. Aim for links on websites that are authoritative, relevant to your business, and trustworthy.

3. **External Location Signals** - 15.5%
   Your listing on the Internet yellow pages, NAP consistency on ALL relevant directories, and number of citations.

4. **My Business Signals** - 14.7%
   Best category for your business, accurate description of your business category, keywords in your business title, proximity to searchers.

5. **Review Signals** - 9.8%
   The amount of reviews you receive from many different online platforms (e.g. Google+, Yelp, Trip Advisor, Facebook, etc.).

6. **Personalization** - 8.4%
   Comprehensive personalization of Google+ accounts connected to your Google My Business profile.

7. **Behavioral & Mobile Signals** - 6.9%
   How visitors respond to the content on your website, including click-through rate, mobile clicks to call, check-ins, offer redemptions.

8. **Social Signals** - 5.8%
   The level of engagement (likes, shares, follows, comments) that your content receives on social networks (Google+, Facebook, Twitter, etc.)

E. Create Your Google Account

You don't need a personal Google+ profile to set-up your local Google My Business page. However, it is recommended that you maintain both. By managing a personal Google+ profile you instantly gain your Google My Business page's first follower and advocate – you! In addition, by building your personal Google+ profile and Circles you gain access to individuals whom you can invite to follow and support your Google My Business page.

Set-up your Google+ profile by visiting: http://google.com/+/learnmore/

F. Setting Up Your Personal Google+ Profile

a. Add People You Know

Google+ will prompt you to add people you know. Search for friends, family, associates, and anyone else in your social and professional circles, and place each within a Friend, Family, or Acquaintance category, or create a new custom Circle that best describes your relationship (e.g. Real Estate contacts). Remember, these are the first people that you will invite to follow your Google My Business page.

b. Follow Things You Love
Google+ will then prompt you to follow your personal and professional interests. Choose categories that suit your personal and professional life.

c. Complete Your Google+ Profile
Google+ will then prompt you to upload a profile photo. Select a clear and professional "shoulders and up" headshot (dressed formally or informally depending on your field of business) no smaller than 250 x 250 pixels. It's important to complete your employment, educational, and residential information. The more complete your Google+ profile is, the easier it is for Google to match relevant users to you and the more people you will be able to invite to follow your Google My Business page.

d. Tell Google+ About Yourself
After completing the steps above you will be delivered to your new Google+ personal profile. First, upload a cover image with an optimum size of 1080 x 608 pixels (no larger than 2120 x 1192 pixels). Then, click the "About" tab and proceed to fill out everything. The more comprehensive the better. Take note to complete the "Links" section, including a link to your website and other relevant online resources pertaining to your business.

e. Join Google+ Communities
Within the "About" section you are presented

with the option to "Discover Communities". Start exploring. Joining Google+ communities relevant to the scope of your business will allow you to connect with prospective customers and clients that have the same interests. These communities allow you participate in discussions and allow you, an authority in your industry, to post content from your website (and your Google My Business page) when appropriate.

Now you're ready to set-up your Google My Business page.

G. Setting Up Your Google My Business Page and Making It Work

a. Getting Started with Google My Business
To get started, visit https://www.google.com/business/?ppsrc=GPDA2 and click the "Get on Google" button.

b. Find Your Business
After clicking "Get on Google", Google will ask you to perform a map search for your business using your business name and address. Google will either recognize your existing business or not.

If Google does recognize your business, you will be asked to confirm your business' name, address, phone number (NAP) and accept the Terms of Service stating that you are authorized to manage the Google+ page for the business.

If Google does not recognize your business you can select "Add your business".

c. **Add Your Business**

After clicking "Add your business", Google will present you with an online form for you to complete. This is where you add your Business Name, County / Region, Street Address, City, Province/State, Postal/Zip Code, Business Phone, and Category.

Ensure that your business name, address, and phone number (NAP) is true and consistent with the NAP found on the contact page of your website. Your address **cannot be a P.O. Box** to count as a local business. It must be a physical location where you conduct business and service customers/clients.

As soon as you start typing into the Category, Google will auto-complete categories. To know which Category to select, search on Google for your most important keyword phrase, and check the Category of the business that is in the top spot of the Google My Business listings – the Seven Pack.

Then check "Continue" once you have reviewed your information for accuracy.

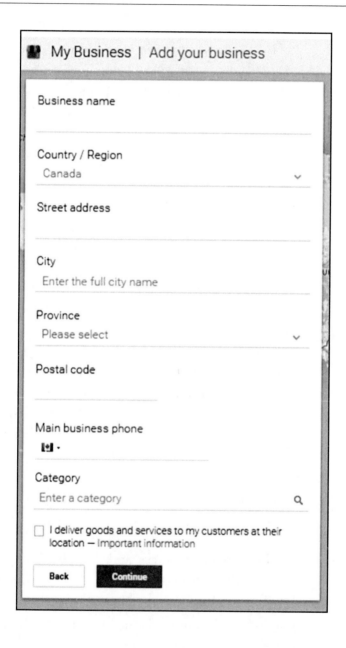

My Business | Add your business

Business name

Country / Region
Canada

Street address

City
Enter the full city name

Province
Please select

Postal code

Main business phone

Category
Enter a category

☐ I deliver goods and services to my customers at their location — Important information

Back   Continue

d. Verify Your Business

After clicking "Continue" and accepting the Terms of Service stating that you are authorized to manage the Google+ page of the business, Google will prompt you to verify your association with your local business. Select and click the "Mail me my code" option.

Within 2 weeks you will receive a postcard from Google that contains a verification code, complete with instructions to return to your Google My Business page to enter the code and verify your local business.

e. **Welcome to Your Google My Business Page**
With your verification code on the way to your local business address you can now begin building your Google My Business page. You can take the tour provided by Google+, or simply continue following this Bonus Chapter to get started.

f. **Adding Your Profile Photo and Cover**
One of the most important elements of your Google My Business page is the imagery used to represent your local business. Your profile photo should be your business logo, no smaller than 250 x 250 pixels. Once you've uploaded your profile photo, it is time to upload a cover image with an optimum size set at 1080 x 608 pixels (no larger than 2120 x 1192 pixels).

Your cover image should be attractive, engaging, and applicable to the scope of your business. Some real estate agents showcase their office, some display their awards, others show members of their team - whatever you feel best conveys the message that your business is trying to send to local customers will suffice.

To follow through on some of the images we've used as examples in this Bonus Chapter so far, here is the cover image of Dandelion Chocolates.

g. **Edit Profile and Complete Important Information**

Once you've uploaded your imagery click the "Edit" button located on the right hand corner of your Google My Business cover. You will be taken to a section that allows you to add additional information that is relevant to your customers.

Add your website URL to your Contact info, complete the Hours of Operation, and add an Introduction. The introduction should be a compelling description of your business that tells people why they should contact you.

h. Verify Your Website and Email

***Verifying your website and email address is one of the most important and beneficial aspects of a Google My Business account from the point of view of your business being found on Google.

Verify Website – Go back to the "About" section of your Google My Business page and scroll down to "Links". You'll see a "Link Website" option beside your website's URL. You can either send the information to your developer/webmaster or you can put the code in your website directly IF you have already set-up Google Webmaster Tools for your site.

If not, you will need to do so (or have your developer /webmaster do it). You may have to seek technical help to place your website verification code in the background code of your website.

Verify Email - To verify your email simply click verify beside your email address on your profile, check your email and click verify in the email Google sent you.

i. **How to Set-Up Google My Business as a Representative in a Multi-Agent Office**

It is very common for real estate agents to work out of an office representing more than one "agent". There may be others in the office that have set-up their own Google My Business local pages. The concern is that Google has stated **there can be no duplication of a business name under the same address**. So how do you work around this? This is how -

1. **Make Sure That the Office Itself Has a Google My Business *AGENCY* Page First**

   There will need to be a Google My Business page set up under the agency brand name, using the local address, general office phone number, corporate logo. The agency website must be verified through the page.

2. **Set-Up Your Google My Business Local Page as an *INDIVIDUAL* Agent**

   Now that your broker's office has a Google My Business page it is time to set-up a page to represent your *personal* brand. In keeping with Google's guidelines on the matter, you must **avoid using the brokerage name as the key identifier in the page.** The local page must be about *you* and **your personal website should be verified** within it.

Of course the address will be the same (that's fine) but the phone number should be unique (your mobile or direct line), and the profile photo should be unique to you. Remember to **link your page and website with that of your broker's page** (and vice versa), under the "About" section within "Links".

Let's clarify here:

Your personal agent page should look like this: John J. Smith, Realtor®

Instead of this: Century 21 Hollywood CA – John J. Smith, Realtor®

Or even this: John J. Smith, Realtor® – Century 21 Hollywood CA

3. **How to Set-Up Google My Business for Multiple Locations**

   If you are a broker you may have a number of locations. In this case, you must use the "Google My Business for Multiple Locations" dashboard, which can be accessed anytime, even after you've created a Google My Business page for your flagship location. The "Google My Business for Multiple Locations" dashboard can be found here:

   https://www.google.com/local/manage/

   Once you've created your first Google My Business local page for your flagship location adding additional locations will be a breeze.

4. **Engage and Post Content Daily on Your**

Google My Business Page
a. Build Circles as a Business

It is essential that you build your Google+ Circles as a local business. Create Circles for *Customers, VIPs, Team Members,* a generic *Following,* and customize additional Circles using keywords to identify them. The more Google+ profiles you add to your Circles, and the more those profiles reciprocate, the greater your audience will be.

b. Join Communities as a Business

Your business should join Google+ communities relevant to real estate or your area of specialization. This will allow you to connect with prospective customers and clients (both B2C and B2B). These communities allow you to participate in discussions and allow you, an authority in your industry, to post content from your website (and your Google My Business page) when appropriate.

c. Post Daily Content as a Business

Once you have built your Google My Business page audience you will have a following in place that is ready to *+1, share,* and *comment* upon the content you post on your Google My Business page.

The more +1s, shares, and comments that you receive on a regular basis, and the more you link this to the content on your website, the more social ranking signals will work to boost the rank of your website on Google. Post engaging, informative, and interesting content on to your Google My Business page daily or as often as you can.

You're almost done! Just a few finals steps towards maximizing the opportunity of Google My Business.

d. Citations and NAP Consistency

A citation is simply a mention of your company name, address, and phone number (NAP) on a website. Adding citations to reputable local online directories is a great way to stay ahead of your competitors. They send authority signals to search engines – so the higher the quality of these citations the better. Especially for the smaller markets, a handful of high quality citations may be all you need to appear to be the best among your competitors.

In addition, Google will look at the name, address, and phone-number (NAP) of each citation to ensure that it is consistent with that found on your Google My Business page/s and the one/s listed on the contact page of your business website. Perform a citation-consistency health check on a semi-annual basis to make sure that it all adds-up. There is software that will do that for you.

e. Here is a list of online resources your local business may be able to get citations on (where applicable):

Yelp.com	YellowPages.com
FourSquare.com	CitySearch.com
Local.Yahoo.com	AngiesList.com
Local.com	UrbanSpoon.com
WhitePages.com	TripAdvisor.com

The entire above process of setting up your Google My Business account and making it work can take as little as an hour but usually requires longer if you are looking for an optimized and well established profile. This could become extremely beneficial to your business.

Be sure to have a fully optimized and well established Google My Business account. There are hundreds of local searches happening in your very own neighborhood every day. Don't let your competitors get all the attention.

JOIN OUR FREE WEBINAR AS A COMPANION TO THIS BOOK –

★ Register Now due to limited number of participants – Go to http://www.topagentinternetmarketing.com/FreeWebinar

"How Top Real Estate Agents are Using the Internet to Capture More Leads and Close More Sales"

- See more Real Life Examples

- Learn Advanced Strategies

- Watch the actual concepts and processes described in this book done for you live

- Qualify for a Free One-on-One Consultation ($500 value)

- Enter your name for a Free Website Analysis ($1,200 value)

ABOUT THE AUTHOR

Ken Lapp has worked in all kinds of advertising and marketing since 1971 - television, newspaper, magazines, billboards, direct mail, promotional items, and print brokering. As well he set up and managed a nationally accredited in-house advertising agency for a large retailer.

He has worked with large retailers such as The Hudson's Bay Company and Army & Navy Department Stores, as well as hundreds of medium and small businesses in every business category. He published the Vancouver Island Tourist Guide magazine for a number of years in conjunction with the Government of British Columbia, which was sent around the world.

In 1999 Ken started Standard Marketing Ltd building world-class websites, optimizing them for search engines, and bringing them customers from Google. Since then he's built an excellent reputation across North America as an ingenious marketing person who understands small business and how to help small business owners make money on the internet.

Over the years Ken helped an increasing number of real estate agents achieve outstanding results with internet marketing. This spurred his partnership with Dan Lok and the formation of Top Agent Internet Marketing Inc., which has now become the flagship of the Standard Marketing group of companies.

Ken says he loves Internet Marketing because it's about customers coming to you when they're ready to buy. I've seen him in action auditing websites, and I can tell you he's one of those rare individuals who knows what looks good, and what will sell.

His business writing receives continuous praise. He's been published in a national Marketing magazine, many websites, and his expertise in marketing for small business is sought out by prominent Vancouver publications, such as Business in Vancouver.

His in-depth understanding of the fundamentals of Search Engine Optimization, his skill at speaking in plain language, and his ability to know how the audience is hearing his message make him an excellent teacher. I heard him say one time "If you can't explain what you're doing in four letter words you don't know what you're doing". His SEO Seminars have always been well received, whether at real estate offices, the Better Business Bureau or local Boards of Trade.

Ken told me once he hadn't had an easy life, but he overcame those obstacles and in the process learned a great deal about himself and other people. This knowledge he's able to put to constant use for the benefit of his customers. He told me one time with a smile, that the only holdover from those dark days is a strong desire to be the best in the business, and help as many people as possible make money on the internet.

As a marketing consultant Ken is phenomenal. More than once I've seen him meet a total stranger during a break at a conference and in 10 minutes be giving the person solutions that speak directly to the heart of their most pressing problem.